# PENNY OVER

## True Adventures of Buying Foreclosures in a Man's World

# Mary Ann Isaacson

Visit website: www.onepennyover.com

Back cover photo by Jennifer Fink,
Generationsbyjennifer.com

Cover design by Jerry Dorris,
www.authorsupport.com

Interior Layout by Jeny Lyn Ruelo
www.thefastfingers.com

ISBN 978-0-9848669-0-8

*Thank you to my husband for listening to these real estate stories a hundred times and laughing at them almost every time.*

*Thank you to my daughters Taylor and Paige for listening constantly to stories of real estate, fixing up houses, construction crews, criminal behavior, and partner woes. You can thank them for your London adventures.*

# Penny Over

## True Adventures of Buying Foreclosures in a Man's World

# Table of Contents

# INTRODUCTION

My husband is from South Africa and was qualified as a chartered accountant. That's the equivalent of a CPA in those tea drinking countries like England, Australia and South Africa. By the time I needed a subtitle for the cover of this book, I was out of clever words, so I asked him if he had any ideas. He came up with some logical, CPA type subtitle that was about two miles long. I was out of creative juice trying to make a deadline, so I said, "Yeah, that's fine," and passed it on to the graphic designer for the completion of the cover. I got a call from that designer when he began his work and he voiced his concern about the subtitle.

I told him, "I hear what you're saying." I knew it was too long and logical and sounded like a CPA wrote it, so we started throwing out some catchy one liners. I tore apart my library of books looking for help. He came up with a few and then I came up with a few. I texted him, "Okay, last one. True Adventures of Buying Foreclosures in a Man's World." He loved it and I thought, *It's good enough, let's get on with it.*

Then I started reviewing the book one last time before it headed off to the editor. In the first few pages, I didn't even realize that I wrote something about being in a man's world. As I was going through the book, I saw that I said it again and I came to the conclusion that somehow, in the hustle and bustle of meeting a deadline, we actually came up with the perfect subtitle. It IS a man's world, especially this real estate arena.

Now that got me thinking. I look at the people who are actively pursuing house flipping as a business. First of all, it's men, men and more men. I think about the ones I've been in meetings with and tried to explain to them that they were either spending too much money or not enough, whatever the case may have been. I tried to put it into terms they could relate to.

"I'm sure you didn't decorate your own house," I said to one of the men in a meeting.

So why do they have such a hard time listening to a female who knows the score? It's not building houses we're doing... it's more like decorating. Yeah, these men have the money to invest in a business of this nature, but who are they? Old macho guys. And I think that's the crux of it. These are the kind of men who made their money in the old school of business. Remember when we didn't even have fax machines? The younger generation, as a whole, are smarter, worldlier and more eco friendly. I remember when our girls were in high school, the boys who would come over would hug each other hello.

I told my husband, "Hey, that's nice, they're a generation of huggers."

But these real estate men are not huggers by any means. Now, I'm no women's libber type, but I still believe that if men are tough, they're great businessmen, but if a woman is, she's a bitch. Well, in my case, it's Ms. Bitch, thank you very much. I don't know if it's because my hair is too blonde, or my boobs are too big, but I can't help that. My rack is real. But the old school real estate guys just don't get it. I'm not giving up on the fantasy that I can someday be treated as an equal in the business world.

Years ago when I turned 40, my elderly mother asked if I felt any different.

"Well, momma," I said. "I've taken 40 years of crap and I'm done with that. From now on, I'm not taking any crap from anyone, unless they're paying me to do it."

She put down her coffee, looked me in the eye and said, "Wait until you turn 80."

## Chapter 1

# HOW I GOT HERE

I look around and I wonder how in the hell I got here, the courthouse steps. It's a combination of the television show Survivor, a huge poker game and being at the DMV. You know, the place where you go to get your driver's license. It's usually a motley crew at the DMV and the same goes for the trustee sales that take place at the courthouse steps.

Sometimes I feel like I'm in a meeting for the United Nations. Someone will be speaking Chinese on one side of me, German on the other side, Russian in back of me, Spanish over there, even Vietnamese and a couple other languages I could never seem to decipher.

Just the other day, one of the guys who speaks Chinese to his investor, who was on the other end of the phone,

13

was bidding. He was telling the other person what the bid was and relaying everything that was happening... in Chinese, all the while covering his mouth and whispering like you would if you didn't want someone to hear what you're saying.

One of the regular guys said to him, "'It's a good thing you're covering your mouth or else we'd be able to know everything you're saying."

Well, it was funny at the time. I guess it's one of those "you had to be there" moments, because the whole crowd, including our Chinese friend, cracked up laughing.

I wouldn't say it's an entirely rough place, but, like that guy Armando says on that house flipping show on television, it's not for the weak of heart, either. The background I came from has unknowingly prepared me for this venture.

I was a real estate agent in the San Francisco bay area for many years and I have the bitchy, suspicious attitude I earned doing it. Working in that kind of environment was like swimming with a bunch of sharks. Actually, that saying isn't completely true with regards to the courthouse steps. At least when you're with sharks, they make no bones about the fact that they want to rip your face off for lunch. Real estate agents you work with want to rip your face off, but they act unassuming and manipulative like they don't. As least with the sharks, what you see is what you get.

I can remember all the plotting and planning involved in trying to get the upper hand in a real estate transaction or listing. Not to age myself, but as long as I'm coming clean, you might as well know it all. At that time, when we presented an offer, it was directly to the seller and the listing agent in person. I remember sitting down and telling the crew sitting across the table from me all the things that were wrong with the property and why the offer I presented had a reduced price. Of course, I did this in the nicest possible way, with an endearing smile on my face. But the point is, it usually brought any seller down from their high horse and many times I was successful.

There was only one time when a seller said to me, "Why do they want the house, then, if it needs so much work?"

I answered, "The location is great and they just want to make the house their own."

*Oh, good answer,* I thought, patting myself on the

back in my mind.

That's one of the advantages I have over a lot of people. I have the ability to think quickly on my feet. My poor husband has a hard time debating with me because I can think of responses to his argument in an instant. Most of the people at the courthouse steps are the same way. If you weren't that kind of person, you'd be chewed up and spit out. Being there for a few years now and buying over 200 houses has really perfected that skill for me. That, and never letting them see me sweat, or never letting them know that they've gotten to me. And there have been plenty of those moments.

That real estate experience taught me lessons you can't pick up in any book, either. I remember many years ago being in a listing agent's office. He was in the conference room with his clients. All of us poor schleps who were trying to present our offers were sitting in the waiting room. All the while, I was sitting there thinking how I was going to get this offer accepted. My mind was working like the gears in a grandfather clock. There were five other agents. I was really going to have to pull out all the stops on this one. I didn't think I had the best offer, either, because even though it was a multiple offer situation, and you should bring your best price, my poor clients could only go up so high.

They were a newly married couple and had just had a baby. The wife was now working part time so she could spend more time at home with the baby. This was going to be their first home and they were looking forward to making it their own where they could raise their family. If you'd like to add violins here, please feel free. Believe me, I laid it on thick and I had no qualms about doing it.

Everyone took their turn going into the conference room and presenting their offers. I just had to hope for the best. I imagined hauling these people around with that darn car seat for the next month. But I was young and had a lot of energy, and the kind of positive attitude that comes with youth, so no sweat. The listing agent listened to the last offer and then the agent who had presented it came out all full of himself like he was sure he got his offer accepted. I slumped a little lower in my chair. Agents can be so darn pompous.

Suddenly, the listing agent came out and asked, "Who's the agent who has the clients with the baby?"

YES! I jumped up out of my chair like I had just won the lottery. Still trying to be cool, I blurted, "Oh yes, it's me."

He brought me into the conference room and told the others they could go, and thanked them for their offers and for coming. Ha, ha, ha. When I went back into the room, I learned that the sellers had been in the same situation as my clients when they bought that house 30 years ago; newly married with their first child. They raised all their children there and now that they all were grown and gone, they were downsizing to a smaller home. It wasn't the best offer, but they wanted to give this young couple a chance. I have never forgotten that story.

In fact, it often comes up in conversation. Of all the offers I've presented and had accepted over the years, that was my first lesson in the fact that it's not always about the money when it comes to real estate. This is invaluable now when dealing with homeowners. It's also one thing I still can't get investors to understand; buying a house isn't always about the dollars and cents for people. This is the place where they're going to make their memories, have their families over for Thanksgiving and maybe bring their new baby home from the hospital. Like that commercial on television says, it's priceless.

Similar to the real estate industry itself, and the plethora of people it attracts, it's an interesting group at the trustee sales, these courthouse people. A guy in town was talking to my husband about them and called them the courthouse rats. I hate to be bundled with that label, but it's not totally off base. You see some of the same faces day after day. It becomes a weird dynamic because you learn to really like some of the people who attend and they help you with information, and vice versa. Then there's the few you would be happy to never see again.

We're like a big dysfunctional family. We fight, bicker and banter amongst ourselves, but let an outsider come to the steps and we collectively gang up on them. I usually feel sorry for new people who don't have a clue and try to help them. I've actually gotten clients that way because I was the only person who would give them the time of day and offer help.

So how did I get here? I suppose out of the few of us who were partners in this new venture, I was chosen by default. We originally had hired someone or contracted them to buy us houses, but that turned out to be a bust. Of course, I've always known about trustee sales, but they were never quite the epidemic they are now. I remember my husband and I were staying in San Francisco one summer while our daughters attended art school. It was a Thursday and CNBC reported that Bear Stearns was in trouble. That sent a shockwave through the stock market, which plummeted around 400 points.

I can remember we had a beautiful flat screen television at my husband's office in the conference room. It would be set to CNBC, which, of course, reported all the stock info for the day. I would go into that room and turn off the television so he couldn't see the sea of red scrolling across the bottom, those scarlet numbers being all the stocks going down in price. He had enough to worry about without that being thrown in his face. It was downhill from then on. Loans started defaulting, there was no money to lend and house prices started to fall, and fall, and fall, and fall.

My husband knew someone who had been buying houses at the trustee sale using investor money and charging a fee. We originally pooled some cash with a partner and bought a house. It was occupied, but that wasn't really the bulk of the problems. We made a good profit, but as you'll read about later, it didn't come easy. Suffice it to say, the guy we paid to go to the courthouse and buy the house for us was not on the up and up, if you know what I mean. I suspected then that the high fix up costs were a result of him getting a kick back. I learned about two years later that he did in fact get money on the side from everyone he hired to work on the houses he managed. We had bought two homes with him and could see the profit potential, but how to get them? My husband had a business to run, so I was unanimously elected. My intelligence began. I started going to the courthouse steps to observe my future competition. I noticed the guys were all holding papers and information that looked like it had been printed out from the internet. I asked someone what website they belonged to so I could see what houses were coming up for auction. Getting some money and going to the trustee sale to buy a house is one thing, but actually doing it and knowing all the policies and procedures is another.

So I went and just started watching everyone. I would hear what information the auctioneer gave when a house came up for auction. I would listen intently to see what bidders said when they were going to bid on a house, what the first one in said, which was typically "Penny Over," what the second one said and so on. I would look to see what they gave to the auctioneer and what was expected of them. I was there for about a week, just observing the whole thing.

If you have this picture of a nice little lady casually watching while everyone leaves her alone, blow it up.

Everyone and their brother were trying to see who I was, what I was doing there, why I was there, and so on and so on. What's your name? Where do you live? Are you buying something today?

"No, I'm just watching," I'd say.

I was there one day when this girl came to the courthouse steps. I say that like it's a big freakin' deal because it is, especially back then, because it was ALL men... and me. She was about 35 or so, and a little rough around the edges. She had a voice that seemed like she was no stranger to a good pack of smokes and a set of double "D"s to go with it. She was talking to a few of the guys and seemed like she knew them and had been there before. She smiled at me and seemed approachable, so I started up a conversation with her. She turned out to be a wealth of information. She told me to stand right next to the auctioneer when I bid. She told me not to let those guys intimidate me, what to say and not to say. To this day, I still stand right next to the auctioneer when I'm bidding. She probably doesn't even know that she gave me such confidence to enter into this man's world, but if she reads this, I owe her a big thank you. She doesn't even know how she helped change my life.

## Chapter 2

# HOW IT WORKS

When I'm at a party or some function, people ask me, "What do you do for a living, Mary Ann?" It's sometimes a loaded question. The foreclosure epidemic in the area I live in is just that. Everywhere you go, people are losing their houses or they're so upside down, meaning that they have no equity left in their house so they make a decision to let the house go to foreclosure. Mainly because of this, I usually try to tread lightly. I don't want the house they lived in to be the last one I bought. Well, if it is, that's one thing, but I don't want them to start wailing on me for it.

But if I try to hide my profession, it can backfire on me. One time I was at a friend's house for one of those dorky parties where they sell stuff that's way overpriced, but you feel obligated, so you buy something. The presenter was taking forever and she was going around the room having everyone give their names and what they did for a living. I'm sure this was some kind of ploy to see who she could recruit to be one of her Betty Crocker type distributors.

My friend whispered in my ear, "This is so boring. Don't say what you really do, say you're a gynecologist."

She knew I was the one with the balls to do that with a straight face and pull it off.

When it came to my turn, I said, "Hi everyone, my name is Mary Ann."

I smiled and paused, waiting for the bait. With those pearly whites that people who don't drink coffee have, the presenter eyed me up and down like a fox in a hen house and said, "And what do you do for a living, Mary Ann?"

Oh, yes, of course, how could I be so forgetful? Ha, ha.

"I'm a gynecologist," I replied like it was no big deal.

Hoooooo. They were impressed and it was written all over their faces. It was all my friend could do to not burst out laughing. The funny part about this boldfaced fib is that for every party I've gone to at that friend's house, the same group is always there.

I went to a party at her house recently and I could hear one of the newcomers say, "Who is that?"

The girl she was talking to said, "She's a gynecologist!"

Oh my gosh. This has gone on for several parties and I don't think I can tell them the truth because I'm afraid they'll be pissed. I'm just glad no one has asked me for a pap smear.

Seriously, though, when someone asks me what I do, I say that I'm a real estate investor or a real estate flipper. Eventually, when we start talking about foreclosure sales, the same question always comes up: "How does that work?"

If you're asking that same question and you bought this book to get some answers, I guess I'll tell you as briefly as possible, then we get on to the good stuff. The way the foreclosure process works, at least in a non-judicial state, is before a bank can take back the property for nonpayment, they have to go through a few steps and one of them is a trustee sale.

In my particular county, the trustee sales take

place twice a day, once in the morning and again in the afternoon. There's a third party website that we all subscribe to that gives a list of the houses that will be up for auction on a particular day.

So, how does it work? That's a bit of a loaded question. There are a lot of pieces to the foreclosure puzzle. If I wrote it all out now, you'd probably tell someone you love this book because it puts you to sleep so nicely every night. But for those anal types, I'll give you a little bit of the who, what, when, where and why.

When there's a notice of default filed on a house, it's done so at the county recorder's office. I'll explain further. Say a homeowner hasn't made any payments for a few months. The bank could choose to file a notice of default on the amount the homeowner is in arrears. A few required months after that notice is filed, if they're still behind on their payments, there's a notice of trustee sale filed with a sales date.

In this day of crazy foreclosures, the issue now is that there are people who haven't made any payments for months, even years, and still no notice of default has been filed. There doesn't seem to be any set pattern for when these notices are filed, but before it can come to the auction, it has to happen.

The seasoned investor or trustee sale bidder will go and look at the property the day before the house is coming up for auction. There's a whole plan of attack on this, but basically they're looking to see if the house is occupied or vacant, what kind of shape the house is in and how much it will approximately cost to renovate. Part of this research might include trying to peek through windows or talking to neighbors to get as much information as possible.

The other thing we look at before we starting bidding on a property is whether the loan that's foreclosing is a first or second deed of trust. Having two mortgages on one home was quite common for a number of years. When you buy a house at auction and it's a first deed of trust and there are second or third mortgages on the same property, the second and third mortgages go away. Basically, the banks that lent the money get the shaft and don't get any payment because the first mortgage gets all the money. The first mortgage is in the primary position and if they're foreclosing, they have first dibs, so to speak. They're taking less than the full amount, so whatever they get, they keep.

If there's a second mortgage on the house and the bank that has the second mortgage is the one taking the house to foreclosure and someone buys it, that usually means they'll lose their money. I say probably because in almost every case now, houses going into foreclosure don't have equity in the property. If they did, the owners would more than likely have sold them with a real estate agent.

The first deed of trust is still recorded on the house and they have precedence over the second or third, and don't go away just because some poor sucker thought he bought a first. That's why the terminology of first, second and third is there. In essence, it states their level of priority. Buying a second deed of trust is probably the worst thing that could happen, short of buying a house that has burnt down... maybe.

Although there was a guy one time who was buying a house and, for some reason, everyone was looking at each other really freaky. I couldn't figure out why and no one said anything to me. I wasn't bidding on that house because I hadn't looked at it. After he got it, someone told me that the house had burned down. But even then, somehow he managed to get the trustee and the bank to give him his money back. Whew. I have never heard of anyone getting their money back because they bought a second.

There was a lady who used to come to the auction every afternoon. She was an older Asian lady and she told me that her knees were bad and she couldn't stand all day, so she only came to the later sale. I did mention that we stand on our feet the whole time, right? Yeah, by the way, when I say I am buying houses at the courthouse steps, I'm not mincing words. It is right on the steps.

Okay, so, getting back to my lady friend. She sort of befriended me because, at that time, she was the only other female besides myself and even though she was a 65-year-old Asian lady who didn't speak very good English, we bonded over our sisterhood. She was there one day and the auctioneer was crying a sale. No, it's not because he was an emotional auction guy. That's what they call it when they do the sale, crying the sale. It's all so antiquated, really. Standing on the freaking steps and crying the sale, who talks like that? Anyway, that's what he was doing.

The lady didn't really jump all over the house. In fact, she sort of hesitated. The opening bid was for some fancy pants house in a top notch area. It was a $750,000 minimum bid. Now, the low end of the bids we usually see are around $100,000 and the high is probably between $400,000 to $500,000, but those are bids that make our heads turn if anyone bids. So, this $750,000 thing was a "whoa" moment. Once again, I hadn't looked at this house or the title info, so I knew nothing about it. I found out later that it was a second deed of trust and she never came back to the auction again. That was about a year ago.

There was another group of people who were apparently big shots. They showed up some time after the Asian lady disappeared. They were there every day and bought quite a few houses. There was a girl buying for this group of investors. She was from San Diego and so the guys there just called her San Diego. I don't even know what her real name was. I don't know what their system was or if she had anything to do with the information gathering, but one week when I was on vacation, apparently she bought two second deeds of trust. One was around $450,000 and the other one was around $285,000! She never came back, but around six months later, they had another guy buying for them, but he eventually pooped out because he said they weren't making enough money. No shit, with that track record.

Sometimes when people show up to watch what's going on, one of the questions they start with is, "Who are the checks made out to?" They want to know how many checks they need to have. The answer is the checks are made out in the name of whoever is bidding on the house. So, if you're going to bid, then the check or checks should be made out to you. If you have someone else bidding for you, the checks should be made out to that person.

Most people at the courthouse are not bidding for themselves. In fact, they've been hired by investors to do the bidding. In many of those instances, the investor will put the checks in the name of their business or LLC (limited liability corporation) and give the bidder a notarized copy of a letter that says they are giving them permission to bid for them and purchase properties. When you buy a house at a trustee sale, the auctioneer has no cash register to give you change, so when we give the check and it's more than the house price, we wait a week or so for the refund.

I'm sure auctions in different counties have different ways of conducting business. I know at our county auction, there is no shade or overhang. There are no chairs to sit on. As I said before, it is literally on the courthouse steps. Usually, the first person in the bidding process will go a penny over. If there is no one interested in the house, the auctioneer will proceed in a fashion that you would assume is the norm. Going once, going twice, third and final time.

Auctioneers handle the last part of the auction in different ways. This sets the table for some of the most tense moments, extreme chaos and name calling arguments I've ever witnessed. Some auctioneers will stop the bidding at the final bid and then give you time to endorse your checks over. Some will not stop taking bids or pronounce the property sold until all the checks are endorsed to the trustee and given to the auctioneer.

So, what happens is, you think the bidding is over and you've got the house. You're endorsing your check or checks and then someone pipes up and bids $100 more. That's typically the way people bid in these auctions, $100 at a time. Once again, nothing is ever typical, though. Depending on how the bid comes out, and who is bidding, it could go $100 at a time, $1,000 at a time, or even $5,000 a few times. I've said before that the auction is a lot like a poker game and you never know what will happen.

You get reads on people and can sense when they're really going for a house and when they're slowing down, or when they're close to their maximum bid. Some may disagree, but I really feel there's a strategy to bidding. Since you're usually bidding with the same people, you get a feel for how they bid, what they'll pay and when they're close to stopping. It's not like we walk up to the courthouse steps and start bidding. There is so much downtime to all of this. You can put that "so much" in capital letters.

So, as a result, you get to know all the players pretty well. You know when they go on vacation, how many kids they have, where they're from, how long they've been married, what they used to do for a living, etc. It's almost like you're going to a job and these are your co-workers. In all those conversations, you get a feel for who's conservative, who's reckless, who's a nice person and who the jerks are.

So, you might be wondering how someone could pipe up after it seems like the house is sold. Most of the people there are working for some investor who has the money, but not the time to stand there all day. So, the actual bidders at the courthouse are usually on the phone with the investor, giving them updates on what's happening with the bid, like what it is and who has it. So when a bid is going up $100 at a time and the bidding seems to be done, they convey it to the person on the other end of the phone.

Who knows what the heck the person on the phone is thinking. There could be half a dozen reasons why they decide they want to continue. Maybe they were reviewing comparable prices again and decided it is worth more than they thought. Or, they might have done all their numbers with a certain amount of fix up costs and at the last minute, they might be thinking they'll skip certain aspects of that or maybe get better pricing from their contractors.

So, many times, the person who is actually there and may be your buddy and not really meaning to screw you out of the house you thought you just had will get the order to bid a $100 more from a boss over the phone. Then the bidding continues and it's not over. I know, this just seems crappy in every sense of the word and believe me, when it happens to you, it sucks. I did it one time and apologized to the guy for a year after because I felt so bad about it.

In my defense, what happened was, I was bidding on a house and it went on for quite some time. It went past what I wanted to pay for it and a fellow real estate agent in the town I work in started giving me info on the house that I didn't know. He said it had been a former model and it had all these built in cabinets and other special things. In fact, he had been in the house before and knew it well. In an instant, I realized that I could probably get $5000 more for the house based on what he was telling me, so I was the one who piped in and said $100 more when the guy was signing his checks. I bid a few more times, but he really wanted the house, so I eventually reached my limit and he won the bidding. I didn't know the guy at the time because he was new there, but we all eventually got to know him and that's when the apologizing on my part began.

With that explanation, you can see how that could create chaos. Not only chaos, but I've seen arguments because people came in at the last minute and someone did get the house, but having to pay thousands more had them seeing red. That's the "tense moments" part, leaving you standing there, waiting for blows to fly. Most of the time, it's not really the fault of the bidder, but the actual investor calling the shots on the phone. When I first came to the courthouse, there was a time when a few of the guys constantly did it for the hell of it.

I don't even know where to begin explaining this one. When I first started buying at the trustee sales, the atmosphere was different than it is now. Currently, it's pretty civil for the most part and you'll learn why later. But, back then in the beginning, there was a cast of characters that were such a bad influence on each other; it was like a high school scene from a Lifetime Television for Women movie. I'm serious when I say they reminded me of bullies on the playground, and to say that is not much of a stretch.

They were the guys who would bid while someone was signing their checks just to be jerks. It was so blatant that it was nerve racking whether it happened to you or someone else. Someone would be signing their checks and one of them would pipe up with $100 more, and laugh and laugh. Their cohorts would also have such a good chuckle at someone else's expense. There was no reason for it and they got nothing out of it. They didn't want the house. They just performed for each other and showed off like junior high kids. It happened to me on more than one occasion and it always happened to new people. A guy I know who went to buy property for himself and a partner got bid up around $10,000 more once the bid was supposed to be over, but he started signing his checks and they got him.

I used to look at those guys, yeah, of course they were guys. Women would never act like that. Not that women are any better, but they're more manipulative and sneaky, so acting like a bunch of idiots showing off isn't really the feminine style.

Anyway, I used to look at them and think that they

looked like the kind of guys who probably got us into this foreclosure mess in the first place. People who have been in the real estate industry for any length of time know what kind of guys I'm talking about. They're the ones between 25 and 35, with that spiky hair, sometimes bleached, sometimes not. These are the kind of guys who were flying high with hummers and big houses with subprime loans. It makes me laugh when I think about it, but it's true. You might be wondering what changed and why it's more civil now than when I first started coming to the courthouse steps. Oh, that's a whole chapter for later.

When someone manages to bid and win a property, either during the breaks or after the auction, the auctioneer will give you a trustee receipt for your purchase. It depends on when they have time. Don't think we get some fancy schmancy pre-printed receipt with a glorious photo of your new property. No, it's more like a crappy 8x11 piece of paper that includes trustee name, contact info, your vesting information and how much you paid, along with some other administrative mumbo jumbo. That's it, that's all you get.

I know it seems ridiculous. You just emptied your bank account and plunked down thousands of dollars, sometimes hundreds of thousands in certain states, and all you have to show for it is a piece of paper that a guy on a step filled out. In about a week or so, they send you a refund if you have one coming and the actual deed from the trustee. When that trustee's deed comes in the mail, we high tail it to the county recorder's office and get it recorded.

"Why can't I go have a hamburger before I record that deed and take my time?" you say. Well, go ahead, take your time and have a shake with that burger. Maybe it's just because I've been a real estate agent for too long. I've seen things happen in real estate that no one could have predicted, so I feel more comfortable having that deed recorded before any questionable liens are slapped on that property, like an IRS, mechanics lien, or anything else. I don't even know what events could take place if that happened, but I'm not willing to sit back and find out. I just know when something is recorded on a property that isn't sunshine and roses, it makes the title company or the lender go, "Hmmmm... not so fast."

Speaking of being a real estate agent for a long time, when I was at the auction a couple of days ago, I was complaining about a client I have who I've listed some houses for. He seems to be sabotaging many of the offers coming in because he's short and has an ego. Ooohh, I feel like I'm tattling right now. It feels kind of good.

I told my young friend that I've been a top producing real estate agent for a long time, and during the recession in the 1990s, I was a leasing and marketing director for a property management firm and I didn't really need this crap, blah, blah, blah.

Anyway, I said, "When I got my real estate license, you were probably in elementary school."

He asked what year I received it. I said 1986.

He said, "I was seven."

Whatever image you have of me and what my face looked like, it's correct, because I went through a few faces in about a minute. Now, if you want to go to the real estate website and look up my license, it shows I got it in 1988. It also shows that it is unofficial and taken from secondary records. One time when I had them on the phone because I had a question about something else, I asked why it showed me receiving my license in 1988 when, in fact, it was 1986. The person told me it was because they didn't have the internet back then and when they transferred the records, they couldn't go back that far in their dates! Uh, okay. No comment!

## Chapter 3

# THE LOAN DEFAULTS

There is a combination of reasons for loan defaults.

You have the borrower who bought a house with no money down and got a subprime loan. This type of loan is basically for borrowers who probably could never afford a house in the first place, and have less than perfect credit. I'm being politically correct here. Let's face it, subprime is for borrowers whose credit is all jacked up. I've heard stories of people like this who got into a loan way over their heads and made one or two payments, then defaulted. Some never even made one payment.

Another is the investor who cash flowed at one time or possibly never did, but banked on the future appreciation. And at that time, future meant a few months. You've probably heard the term, people using their homes like an ATM. Both of those aforementioned borrowers might have fallen into that category. The adjustable interest rate goes up, the tenant moves out and poof, they let the house go.

Sometimes when I'm looking up liens by someone's name, I can tell the investors who had numerous houses; they're all in default or have notice of trustee sales filed on each one. For them, it's more like a business decision. The house went down in value. In our area, like fifty to sixty percent of the value, the cash does not flow, so they give up the house.

I've personally heard of so many tenants who were victims of fleeting landlords.

I knocked on the door of a house that was being auctioned off the next day to talk to the owner to see what their plans were. No one answered, so I started to leave and this incredibly tall man came out with his face furrowed. He wasn't a fat guy. These I know I can outrun. No, he was just, as my daughters say, a beast, meaning he was about 6'5" and really wide and big boned. He looked like one of those guys who would have been a football player in college.

I asked him if he was aware of the fact that the house

was going to a trustee sale. He was pissed, to say the least. I kept talking and tried to help him in his situation as a tenant, giving him his basic rights. He eventually calmed down and even warmed up to me. I found out that he had rented the house in February of that year. I looked at the info sheet I had and showed him that there was a notice of default filed the previous November, which meant the landlord had missed several payments before the November filing and then rented the house to him in February. He had been making regular rent payments to her, and she had obviously been keeping it and not paying the mortgage.

Unfortunately, this has gotten to be a very familiar story. As you'll read about later, it may be unethical, but it's not illegal. I know it should be, but as of now, it's not.

Lately there's been a rush of homeowners who can make their payments, but their house is so upside down in value that they stop making their mortgage payments. I can't say I blame them. I have friends who bought their home for over $800,000 and someone recently moved into a very similar house next door, with a pool and the whole nine yards and paid $450,000! How do you think that would feel? Probably a lot like your balloon lost all its air. They had a very successful business and could make their payments, but it's almost like throwing good money after bad.

Many of these people who see their house upside down in value, but can make their payments, are trying to get their loan modified. This means that they're trying to get the bank to lower their payments, reduce the principle, change their interest rate, or maybe a combination of those factors. Unfortunately, the banks won't listen to a word of your story until you're late with your payment. All of a sudden, they're calling you and want to talk.

The bad thing about that is by missing payments, you leave yourself open to hurting your credit. Homeowners have to decide which is worse of the two: the risk of ruining your credit or being hundreds of thousands of dollars upside down on your mortgage. There's no basic formula in choosing either. It just depends on the individual homeowners and what's more important to them. Having good credit is vital in today's society, especially if you have important events coming up in your life, like your car is about to poop out or you have kids who are going to need student loans to go to college. This is what people are going through every day in this economy and it's definitely not easy for them.

The other thing is that there's no stigma associated anymore with letting your house go. When this all started, it was a big deal if you knew someone who was losing their house to foreclosure, but now there have been so many in our area, it doesn't necessarily mean that someone is financially unstable. It could just be a business decision.

I remember in the late 1980s when I was selling property in what is called the East Bay area of San Francisco. Houses were selling so fast and furious that I would watch the multiple listing service during the day and if I found a house that matched my buyer's criteria, I'd rush out to see it. I would be able to tell if it was something they'd be interested in. I would write up an offer and present it as soon as the listing agent would let me. I'd try and make the appointment at around four or five o'clock before other agents could get their buyers out there. Then I'd write the offer up with an additional term and condition stating that the offer was subject to the buyer previewing the property before 9p.m.

The difference between then and the subprime mess now is that at least these people actually had to qualify for a loan! At that time, you had to have ten or twenty percent of the purchase price to buy a house. I turned so many people away who had less than ten percent to put down because there was just no way to get it done. I remember around 2004, seeing these sheets that the loan representatives would print up, showing that a borrower could buy a house and actually get a loan over one hundred percent. I know, what the heck? What were we thinking? No wonder we got into this mess.

There are also those people who had great jobs and could qualify for their mortgage at one time, but because of the economy, they had to take pay cuts or lost their jobs altogether. They were probably the biggest victims of this housing plunge. They got their loan in good faith and many times could easily afford the payments. Since so many fields and industries are somehow intertwined with the real estate economy, there have been so many jobs lost that have nothing to do with real estate. If you don't have a paycheck, you can't pay your mortgage, plain and simple.

I don't really think about this often because what I've been doing for the last few years is really time consuming and I barely have time to go to the bathroom. But after writing this chapter, I thought about people reading it and wondered if they already had an opinion or if they had developed one over the last few years. Then I started thinking about my opinion on the loan defaults and I pondered what I would say if anyone questioned me. I thought if anyone asked me who I thought was to blame, what would I say? How did I really feel?

I feel like everyone in this mess is a little to blame. There, now everyone can be a little mad at me for taking a side. Obviously, the banks let everything get way out of hand. They were lending money like they were in the back printing it on their very own machine. I'm no fan of the banks, believe me. Someone told me an old saying, which was that banks would lend you an umbrella on a bright, sunny day, but if it was pouring with rain outside, there's no way you'd find a bank to give you one. Why do you think I call them the "banksters?"

The mortgage brokers made loans to people, sometimes unsuspecting, sometimes not, like the end of the world was coming. Back in 2005 or 2006, you couldn't even get a loan person to give you a call back because they were so busy making their own little pot of gold. I know people who made millions at that time. They were flying high with Las Vegas weekends, limos to parties, big houses, fake boobs and fast cars. I would say 95 percent of them have either filed bankruptcy, lost their homes, wives, husbands, and, like my dear departed father used to say, "They don't have a pot to piss in or a window to throw it out." Man, you gotta love those old sayings. So crass, yet so true. Some of these guys would do a loan for a poodle if you could get power of attorney and get it a social security card.

Then there's the borrower who was fraudulent themselves. They knew what they were doing, but fell into the trap of wanting to keep up with the Jones's. They didn't make enough to keep up an apartment, let alone a mortgage, property taxes and insurance, and everything else that goes along with it. Some of these people lied on their mortgage applications because in those "good ole days" all you had to do was state your income. Pick a number, any number, just make it high enough to qualify for this home you can't even begin to afford.

I had a friend who owned a mortgage company at that time. Somehow, she found out that one of her loan officers was falsifying loan documents. I can't remember how she found this out, because that wasn't the memorable thing about it. When I got there, my friend met me at the door, let me in and locked the door behind me. She hadn't told me what was going on, except that I had to get over to her office quick because I wouldn't believe what she found.

"It's not a dead animal, is it?" I squirmed.

"Oh, no, just get over here," she said.

"Is it a live animal?" I uttered in disgust. I'm squirmish about dead animals lying around and even more frightened of one that's alive, ready to pounce on me, or bite.

I rushed over to her office because I like a good drama and wanted to see what all the hoopla was about. She led me into the office of someone who was working there as a loan agent. The room looked like the freaking FBI had been there and tore up the place. She had everything strewn all over the office, separated in piles, and started to explain the situation. This agent had blank letterheads from all the banks. Big banks I won't mention because they'll probably send their goons over to my house, as well as smaller boutique banks.

As if this wasn't enough, she had paper where she had been trying out signatures from different people from the banks. The piece du resistance was somehow she had acquired ink stamps from all these different banks and title companies, and anything else she needed to make something look official. And that shit did look official. Pardon my French. She had been working at my friend's office for over two years, and at the moment, my friend was peeing her pants about all the loans this agent had done with this treasure chest of counterfeit documentation.

So, yeah, I will sprinkle a little of the blame on the loan people and their cohorts, too.

## Chapter 4

# PARDON ME, WHAT'S BID RIGGING?

It's been so long since I've been going to the courthouse steps that I can't really remember when I found out about the bid rigging scheme going on right under my nose. It wasn't like knowing where you were when man walked on the moon or anything like that.

I remember seeing some of the guys walking just a few steps away from where the auction was taking place and getting together in a circle. Now, based on the guys who were doing this, I knew they weren't over there singing Kumbaya. But I was too busy trying to cover my own ass from getting chewed up and spit out by these guys to give it much thought.

I found out that these fellows had their own little auction after the official auction. To this day, I still don't completely know all the details on how they do it, but like the game Monopoly, I know the basics. Here's the unofficial low down.

When a house would come up for auction, these criminals—oh, I'm sorry, guys—would whisper sweet nothings to each other. They would all stop bidding and one of them would win the auction. Say a house that might have sold for $100,000 at the courthouse steps came up with an opening bid of $50,000. When the house went up for auction, a few of the guys would bid maybe $100 more. Then they all stopped and one of them would get the house for maybe $51,000 at the most.

Since they all agreed to stop, it wasn't like the winner was going to get the house for $51,000. He was just the proxy buyer, so to speak. They would then go over under a tree about 25 feet from where the auction was taking place and auction that house again amongst each other. Somehow, and this is where I don't know the particulars, they would pay each other off depending on where they stopped in their own little auction. The person who really wanted the house was getting it for well under the $100,000 potential price and the "circle boys" were getting paid off to stop bidding on the house. And that is bid rigging 101. These guys were making thousands a day practicing this lovely ritual.

The auctioneer knew it, the investors they were buying for knew it and yet, no one seemed to care until one day, but that's a later chapter. I heard from someone who is now buying houses for one of those investors that apparently the investor got in a bit of hot water just for being involved monetarily. I guess the "circle boy" who would get the house in the second auction would tell the investor how much he owed for the pay offs. These are big time, hot shot investors.

One thing I've learned these past few years is how gullible some men are and how these con men can pull the wool over their eyes. I don't think that would happen if they were women. Settle down, we have intuition and we're not afraid to use it.

Well, that just sounds like a good, old fashioned, smart way to do business, you might be thinking. Yeah, maybe in the freaking wild, wild west, but today, we got us some rules to abide by, partner. I believe they call this behavior a felony violation and it could potentially land you a nice room overlooking the San Francisco Bay. It's right down the street from where the bird man of Alcatraz liked to frequent. A little joint called San Quentin Prison.

You see, this is technically stealing money from the banks. As a matter of fact, it was explained to someone on the courthouse steps like this. The FBI considers this type of action in the same manner it would if you walked into a bank with a gun and a note saying, "This is a hold up."

Apparently, the guys involved in this could fool with each other, fool their wives, heck, they could even fool their mommas. But, as they eventually learned, no one fools with the FBI and the banksters.

# Chapter 5

## CAST OF CHARACTERS

The backgrounds of the crew at the trustee sale probably aren't what you'd expect. Since the pace is fast and there are numbers and checks flying around and strategies to think about, these people tend to be smart. Many of them are very well educated, including a couple with MBA degrees, and those without education are very savvy and street smart.

Since I began purchasing homes at the trustee sale, I'd say I must have seen around 100 different faces. For the most part, though, there are probably around 12 regulars who are fierce competition. Some of these guys I've never bid against because they have different areas of interest than mine. I'll give you the run down on some of the bigger characters.

# WINSTON

Winston is what I'll call him. He looks like a cross between Winston Churchill and Santa Claus. He doesn't really seem like a drinker, but he's got that ruddy look to his face like someone who's pounded back a few at the local pub in their day. He's round and jolly and his clothes always look like he's slept in them... for about a week.

Of course he has a strong English accent and is a complete character. He's always talking and never listening. Because the trustee sale process is so archaic and is literally on the courthouse steps, there are so many distractions, like cars speeding by, horns honking, people talking and babies crying in their strollers. There are train tracks with a full on station a couple blocks away and if I didn't know better, I'd think the street in front of the steps was a training ground for bikers trying to get into the Hell's Angels. It's all the noise and drama you would find at a superior courthouse in an urban environment... or at your local discount store.

Because of all of this, when the auction is going on, you really have to pay attention and listen intently. Our buddy Winston never listens and, as a result, is always asking in the middle of the sale, "Say, what was that address?" or "What did you say that minimum bid was, old man?" to the auctioneer. You know, like an English bloke would do. We all laugh and have come to expect it. Nobody really cares, except when the rain is pouring down on us or it's boiling hot and we want to get the show on the road.

The story about Winston goes that he's as rich as Roosevelt. Apparently he owns hundreds of rentals, mostly in an area outside of San Francisco that is really, really bad. It's probably got one of the highest crime and murder rates in the Bay Area. This is why he drives a car that looks like it's on its last leg, so he can get in and out of the area unnoticed. It's got no less than three different colors on it, including that gray mat primer they put on cars before they paint them. It's some sort of old, boxy, small thing that the model name plate came off of years ago.

I remember one day when I came to the trustee sale, I was early and it hadn't started yet. I was walking down the street and I saw that piece of crap car parked with Winston inside. I recognized him even though I had only been going there for about a week or so. He's pretty much one of a kind, so it was easy to recognize him. I looked inside and I could see him sitting in the driver's seat. Not only did the car look like it wouldn't make it down the street, but, to make matters worse, the inside looked like it would be owned by one of those people on a hoarders show. He had clothes piled in the back seat, folders and papers everywhere and in the condition he kept it, even though it's a five seater, you'd probably only be able to fit two and a half people in it.

So I bent down to take a closer look and saw that his eyes were closed. In fact, he didn't look like he was breathing. I was pretty concerned because of his age and the fact that he was sitting far from the steering wheel, but his tummy was touching it, so he wasn't in the healthiest shape. I was the new kid on the block and didn't want to focus any attention on myself yet, so I figured I would mention it to someone when I got to the courthouse steps. I mean, if he was already dead, what was the rush? When I got there I saw a nice gentleman I had met before who was one of the regulars. I told him that I had seen Winston in his car with his eyes closed and it didn't look good.

"Oh, don't worry," he said, "he takes a nap in his car before the afternoon auction."

Winston is there most days. He's not mean or

irritating like some. When seeing someone who hasn't been there for a while, he'll say with a completely straight face, "Where've you been, in jail?"

I'm not sure if he's serious or not. Whenever a new person comes to the steps, Winston is the spokesperson for all of us. Of course, we're all curious, but everyone stands around and looks at the newbie and tries to figure them out. Winston gets all up in their grill. I mean, all up close and personal. He'll ask with his head cocked to one side with that damn English accent what house they're interested in or did they just buy that house as a rental or flip? Or what do they think that house is worth? He's about as subtle as a bull in a china shop.

Plus, the way he dresses is distracting. He's usually always in shorts, even on rainy days. Along with the huge tummy, he wears black or brown knee socks with dress shoes. You know the kind that lawyers and CPA's wear? Yeah, okay, he wears them with shorts.

One day, it was really hot and he showed up with his shorts, black dress shoes and socks, and a red polo type shirt. Usually all his shirts look like he's had a good meal and worn them a few times after that. This one looked like either he had gained a few pounds since he purchased it, or he washed it and it shrank a few sizes. Either way, his tummy was peeking out of the bottom and he gave us all a good laugh. On those hot summer days, because the sun can be blistering, he also sports a big straw hat. Hey, I can't make this stuff up. Yes, Winston wears his attire proudly.

# JAIME

I originally thought that Jaime was of Mexican decent and for all I know, he really is. This is like a New York schoolyard at the courthouse and you can't really believe what anyone tells you. Calm down if you're from New York, you know it's true. Even the good guys might have the wrong information because it's fed to them by the bad guys.

I later learned that he was of Columbian ancestry. In fact, one summer, he went back to visit Columbia for a few weeks. He's probably reading this and laughing his ass off because he really is from Guadalajara and he faked everyone out. I'm afraid the characters part of this book is like one of those unauthorized biographies where it's all hearsay and nothing can be verified. At least I've changed the names.

Jaime doesn't buy houses for himself, he buys for an investor. He's like a Mexican jumping bean all the time. It's more than just ADHD. He seems to be pretty focused, but just has this tremendous amount of energy to burn. So he ends up going from step to step, back and forth, bidding and jumping from group to group. He's a pretty young guy who is somehow connected with one of the heavy hitters of the courthouse steps. He told me that the guy was his stepdad, but once again, he could be shitting me and could have just found the job on Craigslist.

The funny thing is after the whole separation of good guys and bad guys, which I'll talk about later, he came back and we became allies. I don't know how it happened, but even though he isn't completely of moral fiber, I like him.

If he reads that last line, he would look at me puzzled and say, "Hey, what you talkin' about?"

He's funny and witty, and it's nice to be friends with a bad ass. I didn't say if that was me or him. Ha.

# BARNEY

One of the particular fools at the courthouse steps stands out because of his mindless rantings. I'll call him Barney. I've actually done business with this guy in the past. I'm sure you know someone now or have run across someone like this in your life. If not, beware of the Barney type. First off, he's short and slight in stature. I apologize to you short men for this, but we women, and some men, know you can't be short without having short man's complex. In fact, I've made it a life goal to find one. Other variations include little man's complex, short guy syndrome and so on.

To add to the short guy theory, my college age daughter would say I'm generalizing and perhaps I am. But explain this to me. Why is it that the biggest, tallest car or truck is always driven by a short guy? Next time you see someone get out of one of those 10 foot, off the ground, bright blue or red trucks with the tires on it that look like they were stolen from a big rig... think of me, because chances are it's a short guy who's going to jump out of it.

These guys are the same in every town or city across the US, probably the world. Heck, look at Mussolini or

Napoleon. They were short guys. The short guy is often times loud and obnoxious. They can be those in your face kind of people. You know, like those little Chihuahua dogs. Short guys are probably reading this and getting all fired up. I wish I could see them.

Barney is a jokester at the expense of others. He's full of himself when he has his posse around him. He's the epitome of someone who is all talk when the gang is around, but when he's alone, he has nothing to say. It's pitiful, really, but annoying, nonetheless.

Unfortunately he hasn't limited his bantering to my benefit. It seems like his nature is to pick on the less fortunate, or perhaps those who won't answer back..

One day, a young girl came out of the courthouse near where the auction was taking place. She was obviously in emotional turmoil because she was visibly shaken. She was heading in one direction and what seemed like her two small children were going in another. Whatever the girl was or had become to be losing her children was perhaps her own fault, but you can't help looking at that scene and feeling nothing but sorry for her and her children as they were separated.

Our buddy Barney began laughing and pointing

because she was crying loudly and carrying on. I was glad when the other guys standing with him just shrugged their shoulders with indifference. I think they felt bad and didn't want to be part of these childish antics.

I spoke to one of the decent guys at the courthouse, who is a regular bidder, about Barney and told him how he had begun resorting to calling me names. I know... I am talking about a grown man, though it doesn't seem like it.

This regular began his comments to me by saying, "Well, you know he has little man's complex."

It was all I could do to not roll down the courthouse steps with laughter. My own theory proven by someone else.

When you're notorious, everyone has a story about you. Here's one about Barney. One of the guys from the courthouse steps, who is also a real estate agent in the city I'm in, told me that they had bought a house at the auction and it turned out that there were people living in it. That might be a stretch to say, because my friend said that when they went to inspect the home, there was nothing in the closets. No clothes, no shoes, nothing. They had some mattresses on the floor and a chair or two in the living room. It was a very nice, large, newer home. It was probably $3,500 square feet and I remember I went and saw it when they listed it after the people were out. It was one of the nicer homes I'd seen in this area. It was a beautiful one story, with columns and pillars very tastefully done. The floors were hardwood and granite and tile was everywhere.

My friend said that when he went to talk to the people who were living in the house after they purchased it, they were very evasive about what they were going to do and where they were going to move. Apparently, it took a lot of coaxing, but they finally agreed to move to another rental. My friend agreed to some kind of monetary exchange for them moving out. The people told him where they were moving to and he knew the property manager who was renting out that house, so instead of giving the deadbeats, oh, I'm sorry, I mean squatters, oh, I mean tenants, the money, he made a check to the property manager and gave it to him directly. After all, that's what the money was for, right? After, they moved out, the property manager called my friend and said that the people never did show up to rent that house and he still had the deposit.

My friend said that after this episode happened,

Barney, who had been bidding against them on that house, was all over them. Bidding them up for houses he didn't even want and just basically razzing them as the good old boys do. My friend said he always felt that Barney had broken in and moved those people into the house so others wouldn't be interested in bidding. This isn't the first time I've heard this story connected to Barney. Like Arsenio Hall used to say, things that make you go hhmmmmm.

# JOHN LITTLE BALLS

With all the banter going back and forth, there was one day when Barney really pissed me off. I can't even remember what was said, but it had something to do with me staring him down and saying that I had bigger balls than him or a stupid comment like that on my part. I'm not proud of it, but if you can imagine all the days of facing his wrath, there had to be a couple of times when I said something. It only happened once in a while and I could count the times on one hand.

So this day that I piped up, John Little Balls happened

to be standing right next to Barney. When I gave the evil stare down, and some ranting about him having little balls, he thought I was talking to him. Poor guy. He was one of the good guys who happened to get stuck in the bad guy circle. He is under 30 and buys a house here or there, but is very often at the steps, or I should say, he used to be there quite often. Suffice it to say, he's a shorter guy like Barney and he took it personally, even though it wasn't meant for him. From that day on he became John Little Balls...well, in my house anyway.

## BIG TALL WALT

This guy is like a Greek god, except he's tall, gorgeous and not Greek. His skin is a dark honey color, like someone who has a beautiful tennis club tan, only his is natural. Walt is the kind of guy everyone drools over. The girls go gaga over him and all the guys want to be him and have a physique like him.

When I say he's tall, I'm not just saying the guy has a little bit of height on him. He's around 6'9" and built like a brick wall. One of the guys at the courthouse said he wished that he could just have his broad shoulders. You know you're hot stuff when straight guys start saying stuff like that about you.

He shows up with designer sunglasses, clothes and a different car for each day. He's got those beautiful light green eyes and a charming personality. That's probably not a true description of his demeanor. Now, I mean this to his credit when I say that he is so funny he literally has us holding our stomachs in stitches.

One day, I was there for the entire day, from around 9:30 in the morning to 4p.m., standing in the hot sun. That guy entertained us so much that it got all of us in such conversations I left empty handed, but saying to the guys that I had such a great day, even though I didn't even buy a house. He's one of those people who can tell a story in such a way that it is hilarious, like a comedian does.

Walt used to be a professional basketball player and I think it was in some professional European league. I don't even know if there is such a thing, but Walt is one of the good guys, so if there's somewhere in Europe where you can play basketball, I'm sure he did it. As a result, he has all of these incredible stories about traveling all over the world.

One stands out about him playing in some pro European kind of tournament. I think he said it was in Italy. He said that when they won, the fans rushed the court, which was a field that had been transformed. He said it was so frightening because there were hundreds of people running toward the players so star struck that they were ripping off their clothes as souvenirs. He said that by the time he got to the locker room, he was butt naked.

I asked him, "What about your shoes?"

"Butt nekkid," was his reply.

When an auction sale is taking place, most people bidding will huddle around the auctioneer in a tight circle to see and hear him. If you have ever been to a little kid's party, it's exactly like that. The mom makes all the kids sit in a circle a short distance away from the birthday kid to give him or her space to open his presents. But as the packages start to be opened, those kids ease closer and closer to get a better look. We do the same thing around the auctioneer as soon as he opens his mouth with a bid, except for Big Tall Walt, who stands on the lower steps looking down at the auctioneer over the back of everyone's heads.

# SHORTER GREEK WALT

This can be confusing at times. Both named Walt and, as my husband has said in the past, they are like chalk and cheese. I don't know what the heck that even refers to, but it's some English saying, which means two people are completely different. I don't know why they don't just say that, but don't get me started on how the British English and American English languages are so different.

Walt works for a big conglomerate of a company. They are some high profile ex-athletes who I've never heard of, but all the men are like... ooohhh. So I guess they're legit. I hope they don't read this because they'll be insulted, but I don't mean to be insulting. I just don't follow sports that closely to know everyone's name, past and present, except maybe Joe Montana.

Walt is like a breath of fresh air. He's a very, very nice guy. Unlike the Greek god, Walt, this one is just plain Greek with one of those last names with a lot of K's and S's. He doesn't look like what you would envision a Greek would look like. He has very light, olive skin with straight hair and the paunch that comes with the age of 50. He's one of those guys who I think people don't realize how smart he is. If you get to know him, though, you'll find out he has had an interesting life. He even owned some biker kind of bar in Northern California and has some great stories from those days.

# VINCE

Vince is an older dapper gentleman. He always wears nice slacks and a dress shirt. He's got curly strawberry blonde hair and is about six feet tall. He is also a real estate agent and works for some guy with very deep pockets. Vince was one of the only guys who was friendly to me when I first started going to the auction.

I was hanging around for a few weeks and finally bought something.

He said to me, "What is your name?"

I said, "It's Mary Ann."

"Oh, that's going to be a problem and I don't think that's going to work."

"Pardon me?" I was confused.

He said he had a mean, fat aunt when he was growing up and her name was Mary Ann, so they couldn't call me that. I like how he grouped the other guys into his ambivalence towards poor Aunt Mary Ann.

"How about Mary?" he said.

"Fine," I agreed.

I was thinking, *I don't care what they call me as long as they leave me alone and let me buy houses.* At that point, I could see the bad guys picking on anyone they could. Vince wasn't one of those guys. He was cordial to everyone and he was well respected by everyone there. He would help anyone who needed help by handing them his clipboard to sign checks or passersby who needed directions.

He was indirectly involved in some of those illegal courthouse shenanigans I'll talk about later, simply by being employed by someone who was actively participating. I never asked Vince how old he was, but he said that he had a daughter who was 37, so I figured he was in his early 60s.

# HARRY

Harry is a young Chinese guy who speaks the equivalent of Spanglish. If you're not familiar with that term, it's something they speak in California. It's a combination of English and Spanish. It seems to be really prevalent with the younger Hispanic community. So I guess what Harry speaks to his investor on the other end of the phone most of the time is Changlish.

For this reason, we can usually figure out what the heck he's talking about because he mixes the Chinese up with street names and trustee information. He speaks with a pretty strong accent and when he is asked a question or, for that matter, when he asks one himself, he always stops and looks at you with a long pause, like he is pondering the moment. He nods his head when he talks or is listening like a rooster. At least I figure he's listening to me when I talk with that acknowledgement, so as far as Harry is concerned, he's cool with me.

# MILT

This goon works with my old partner. He's got one of those shaved heads, a big gut and chicken legs. I know

I'm no Cindy Crawford, but when you have one of those weird body types, it doesn't matter what you do, you look funny. He has this way of walking with his chicken legs really far apart. Maybe that's to accommodate for the tummy.

Since we're from the same city, I remember meeting him at a coed poker tournament at the real estate agent's house we were using to list all of our properties. It was a nice, friendly event and I remember he got shitfaced drunk. Not just tipsy and slurring words. He was belligerent and was really mean to his wife. Someone had to take him home and put him to bed. I remember I didn't like him then. I don't care about the shitfaced drunk thing, but he was one of those guys who thought he was all that and clearly wasn't, so he had to take it out on his poor wife. If that was my husband, I'd kick his ass, but that's probably another book.

I remember when we were looking for someone to help us with the construction supervising, our real estate agent, who is his friend, suggested this guy. You'll meet that guy later in the book. His name is Kiss Ass Real Estate Agent.

"He IS my friend," Kiss Ass Real Estate Agent said, "but I don't really like him."

He went on to say that the guy had been fired from every job he's ever had. The last job was with a large retail business. Allegedly, he had jerked around the guy he was in charge of so badly that the guy said fire him or I'll sue the company. Man, I wish I had power like that. So, they canned Mr. Chicken Legs.

Now he's buying homes for my old partner, which makes sense, because my old partner loves to hire people who are incompetent and push them around until they reach their breaking point and kiss his ass the whole time. Chicken Legs doesn't have a pot to piss in, but he does have a house under water to throw it out. So my old partner has this guy buy the houses at the auction, pays him shit and charges the investors thousands for doing it, and then gets Kiss Ass Real Estate Agent to give him back half of his commission just for the pleasure of receiving his listings. A match made in heaven.

# JURGEN

This is a fun one. Well, Jurgen isn't fun at all. In fact, just the opposite He's a typical stereotype of a stern

German who never smiles. He's very smart. In fact, he graduated from one of the top universities in the US in business. I happen to know that this school is very hard to get into.

Jurgen seems to know a lot about current events and worldly topics. I think that's pretty normal for foreigners, though, because if they're from somewhere else, they've usually traveled more than Americans. I like Jurgen and have had many conversations with him. He's just a straight, to the point, functional German, kind of like my Mercedes. I think he even drives an older one.

During my courthouse tenure, my eyesight for reading up close was getting really shitty. During the winter, it was okay because I didn't need sunglasses, but when summer came, around I found myself switching every 30 seconds from sunglasses to reading glasses.

I said to Jurgen, "I guess what I need is one of those chains for my reading glasses, but I don't want people to think I'm an old lady."

Of course I was kidding and waited for him to tell me I didn't look that old.

He looked at me with no expression and in a thick German accent said, "It ages you ten yeahs."

I just looked at him. I didn't know whether to thank him or slap him, but I never will get one of those old lady chains.

# MATTHEW

I guess Matthew would be the American as apple pie version of Big Tall Walt. He's not as tall as Walt, but he's not short at all. He's close to being tall, dark and handsome. If I had to guess, I'd say he's somewhere around 30. Way too young to be such a jerk. Matthew is very handsome. If he was taller and thinner, he could probably get modeling jobs. I say that with trepidation because he's been the ring leader in most of the bullying that's gone on at the courthouse steps. He's crass and loud and swears, no matter who's around to hear him.

Matthew was very proud of the fact that he ruled the roost at the trustee sales. With the chaotic nature of how the bidding wouldn't stop until all of your checks were signed, it definitely helped to be on the right side of the auctioneer.

One time when someone got a house at the last minute

and outbid Matthew, he got mad at the auctioneer and said, "What the hell am I paying you for?"

I had heard before and after that our beloved auctioneer guy for the morning sales was on the take and this just confirmed it.

Somehow, Matthew got investors to give him a bunch of money and it seems that it really went to his head. Millions of dollars can do that to a person. This guy would blatantly pick on new people in an effort to try and chase them away and therefore eliminate competition. He would also taunt the regular attendees by placing bids at the last second on houses he really didn't want, just to make the price go higher. They call this bidding someone up.

They even do it on that Storage Wars show on television. Why anyone would want to buy someone else's crap that they have to sort through is beyond me. They can come and go through my shit and I won't even charge them to take it away.

I saw this bidding up thing happen many times and it would be quite uncomfortable, but, as luck would have it, it seems karma will be coming come back to bite our Matthew in his cute little butt.

Soon after my being at the trustee sales, I decided I should implement that old age adage of keeping your friends close and your enemies closer. I would banter back and forth with the guys, including Matthew.

"Good morning, Matthew," I would say. "How's it going?"

I guess he started to feel comfortable with me because I remember one day after I had been there buying houses for a few months, Matthew came up to me with Jaime. They were acting very secretively, but did this in front of everyone.

"So, we can see you're not going away," he said reluctantly.

"Uh, yeah, it doesn't seem so," I said.

The next few words out of his mouth were basically asking me to be in on the inner circle. I knew this was not a circle I wanted to be in because, as I told my husband, I like silver bracelets, just not when they're connected with a chain, if you get my drift. But I was nervous, leery and chuffed with myself all at the same time. It's kind of like having one of the so-called Mafia guys ask you to be part of their family.

I said, "Yeah, we'll see how it goes. I'll keep you posted. What the heck? Might as well."

I was rambling and had to get out of that fast. I mean, you don't exactly say no to the mafia guy, but you just don't show up to that restaurant with the red and white picnic tablecloths. As it turns out, not going to that restaurant was one of the best decisions I've ever made.

# JEFF

Jeff hasn't been around for quite a while and here's why. He was working for some investor when apparently, as the story goes, Barney offered him the moon to come over and steal, oh, I'm sorry, I mean work with him. I think he did this because Jeff was working for someone Barney had previously been working for and it ended up with sour grapes. What a shocker.

Seeing the two of them together was really a sight. Jeff had been a professional football player and even had a super bowl ring. He was freaking huge. You know in the beginning of those Sunday football games on television when they show the player lineup? Those starting guys usually have those really square heads and no neck. That was Jeff. So the fact that Barney needed a stool for the bar made for some funny double takes.

With the help of some free online advertising, Jeff allegedly was breaking into houses that were vacant and in foreclosure, changing the locks and then renting them out. Ahhhh. Can you believe the gall? Apparently, people were giving him first, last and the deposit in cash and he posed as the owner of the house.

I don't know all of the gory details, but my husband was reading the paper one day and said, "Hey, do you know a guy named Jeff?"

Whoa. There was his big starting lineup mug in the paper. The local police had arrested him because someone had called them when the whole deal didn't pass the smell test. They arrived at the house he was trying to rent to unsuspecting tenants and they gave him a lovely set of silver bracelets and a ride to the county jail.

# NATASHA

I got the feeling that Natasha was a true blue slum lord. The houses she bid on were all in that crime ridden area I spoke about earlier. Plus, they were really the low end price of that city, so I can only imagine the kind of places she was buying. She was around 60 and had a strong Russian accent. Once in a great while her husband would come and hang out with her. They would spend the time speaking with a lot of sentences that had "da, da" in them.

You know whenever a woman shows up, we sniff each other out like two new puppies and this was no different. I really enjoyed talking to her, especially since everything she bid on I wouldn't be caught dead going after.

# STEVE

Steve is one of those great guys. He's someone I don't mind losing a house to. He comes most days to the auction and always arrives early, unlike me, who rushes like a mad woman, jumping out of my car and looking down to make sure I put on all my garments before leaving home. He parks in the same one or two spaces right at the bottom of the courthouse steps every time.

Steve is a really good person, but very competitive. He holds a record for being the fastest person to ever water ski barefoot and he's really a jock. He's always bitching when someone beats him out of a house and says they paid too much.

One day, Big Tall Walt said, "Tell me, Steve, how is it that they paid too much, but you were going to pay $100 dollars less and that would be okay?"

Then Big Tall Walt went into one of his comedy shows about how Steve is always complaining about people paying too much, but it's only $100 more than he was willing to pay. I swear, that guy should be on television.

# DON, KARL AND LIAM

I actually went back after this book was done and added these three musketeers. These are three of the good guys and I can just hear the bantering about how I didn't include them. And, how they could tell who was who and they can't believe I would leave them out of my book and put in all those criminals. I'd hear about it for months to come, and anytime anyone mentioned the book. Believe me, I know these crybabies, so here you go.

## DON AND FRED

These two work together. On the down low, we share lots of information, but I don't think anyone knows that about us. They are really nice guys; in fact, some would consider them dorks. Personally, I fancy a dork for conversation, so I'm okay with that. I trust them completely and they would be the first two I would have hold my cashier's checks if I had to go potty and couldn't bring them with me. The checks, not Don or Fred.

# KARL

Karl is a real estate agent in town. He's about six foot four and a big guy. When he first showed up at the auction, he had kind of a scowl on his face, so I thought he was a crab and didn't pay too much attention to him. Once I got to know him, I realized that he's a nice guy and one of the good ones. It just goes to show, you should never judge a book by its cover.

## Chapter 6

## FIXING THEM UP

My husband recently met with the owner of a well known home building company. The home building business is pretty much in the toilet in many parts of California and the rest of the country. It's probably one of the reasons there's quite a few homebuilders jumping into the flipping business.

When he and my husband were going over all the details and getting to the particulars, like who is going to fix up the houses, my husband assumed that since this guy was in the home building industry, he would want to pull a crew from his business and have them work on the houses. I got the idea that he was a really smart man because he said that if a builder worked on fixing up houses, you would never be able to make any money. I couldn't agree more, and so the story goes.

As I said before, my husband and I had done quite a few flip houses before we went to a guy my husband used to work with and showed him what we were doing. He had access to some investors who were looking for a place to put some money because you can now get squat for interest from banks. Initially, he didn't like the idea because of the taxes he'd have to pay. I swear, some people can't see the forest for the trees. He had gotten this investor money and he was buying rentals for cash off the MLS. We told him that buying rentals was great, but he was going to run out of money soon, because you put a tenant in the property and then you're stuck with that house for at least a year while the tenant is living there. Nope, he wasn't interested, so we kept on with what we were doing.

My husband saw him some time later and he asked how the flip business was treating us. This was in the early stages and the profit margins were enormous. We gave him some examples of what we had done and lo and behold, Mr. Greedy wanted in. I love all these cute nicknames everyone has.

The good thing about this partnership was that he brought even more money to the table from his investors and he had a share in a construction company. It sounded great because the construction crew he could put together could do anything and we would probably save money on that part of it because we had an in like that. Ha, ha, ha. How wrong we were.

The first house we bought with them needed a lot of work, mostly clearing out of all the crap left behind. They started working on the house and I bowed out because I was going to focus my efforts on finding more houses that we could buy. Hey, this made sense to me, let the construction guys deal with the fix up.

When they asked me to go take a look at it after they were well underway, I walked into the house to find that the mustard type of color that I had chosen for the house was everywhere! They had painted this color on the ceilings, the baseboards, the doors, even the banister leading to the second story was painted mustard. This is a great color and looks good on walls because it's very chameleon like, looking good with many different types of tile, granite, and carpet, but they had painted every inch that needed painting with this color. I walked through the house in shock. At the time, I didn't realize that this wasn't going to be the last time I would walk through one of the houses shaking my head.

The person who gave the go ahead to paint this house

like a Disney ride was actually the superintendent. Yeah, the guy who was supposed to be in charge of the construction crew was indeed a moron. When I kindly told him that I thought the house would be much better without yellow doors to every room, he was kind of insulted. It wasn't even a matter of opinion, it was ridiculous to think that anyone would think this looked good, except maybe a blind guy. So, they had to have the painter repaint the trim, baseboards, doors, ceilings and banister a nice white ivory color, which is what it should have been in the first place. Of course, this was an extra expense because it wasn't the painter's fault; the boss was a moron.

When that house was finished and our partner was going over the invoices, he asked me if I had approved a charge for the cabinets to be painted for $2,900.

"What the hell?" I said. "You know how cheap I am. Does that sound like something I would do?"

He agreed it didn't sound like me because when it comes to fixing up these houses, I have great common sense. I tried to explain the fix up to someone with this analogy: A big department store like Macy's won't buy the same type of clothing for their San Francisco or Los Angeles stores that they would buy for their Milwaukee store. Companies are paid millions for their demographic research. So many things play into that, like weather, income and location.

The same goes for the fix up on these houses. Some of them are in really nice areas, some are a bit ghetto. I bought a house for an investor in an area that was lower income, but not the worst around. The contractor he had hired was taking out the linoleum and putting in the most beautiful tile in the kitchen and bathrooms. The original floors were fine, especially for that area. I just shook my head because I tried to tell the investor that he was spending unnecessarily, but for some reason he didn't get it, so I gave up.

I soon figured out that the prices we were paying my partner's construction company were three times what I had been paying before. I tried to get him to use another crew that wasn't part of his company, but he resisted big time. At the time, we were making so much money, it wasn't really worth the fight. But, as I figured out a year or so later, using his own construction crew was part of a grand plan for him to make more money on bullshit fees and pad the construction costs behind my back and right under my nose.

One of the next few houses with Superintendent

Moron in charge was even more of a disaster than the first one. By now, my partner could see that it was costing him a lot more, even with all of the schnitzeling fees he was receiving from his naïve investors. We kept on begging him to take this guy off the jobs, but it wasn't until the middle of this next house fix up that he finally did.

I bought a house for us in a very nice area. It was a fantastic, executive style house that backed up to open space, which was a huge regional park and would never be built on. This was a big plus for us in the San Francisco Bay Area because it's so congested, especially in the suburbs. The house was on a lot that was over 15,000 square feet, another show stopper in our area.

The house itself was 4,239 square feet. I remember this because the interior was another thorn in my side. This house had marble flooring downstairs and a floor to ceiling fireplace in the family room. It had plantation shutters everywhere and it didn't even look like anyone had lived there, at least not for very long. It was in great condition and included all the stainless steel appliances for once.

The house was built around 2006. That, combined with the fact that it was in such good condition, made it seem like a new house. The people who must have owned it didn't do anything to the backyard except put in a pool, but there was no landscaping to speak of.

Superintendent Moron was a pretty old geezer with gray hair and really white and pink skin, the kind that looked like he hadn't turned down any alcoholic drink that had been offered to him. He had a pretty average build and average weight for his age. He lived about two or three hours away and didn't have a clue about our area, or anything else for that matter. The guy did manage to use a cell phone, but didn't text. In my opinion, if you can't communicate via text, you should just stay home and bake cookies or move to a retirement community.

My partner, who was deathly afraid of any kind of conflict, had us all meet at his office to discuss this house because they were going way over budget and I was ready to tell them why. His partner in the construction company was also there. The partner was in his early sixties and basically a hick from a hick area. You know you're a hick when you live outside of the Bay Area of San Francisco and the town or city you're in isn't even considered part of that area. I tried to explain this guy to someone one and I was having a hard time.

I got a few words out and the guy I was talking to

said, "Oh, he's one of those hicks with a big gut, cowboy hat and no ass."

*He nailed it,* I thought. *When did he meet this guy?*

So, there we were in my partner's office to talk about the fix up of that beautiful house.

Superintendent Moron and No Ass guy said, "That backyard is going to cost at least $50,000."

I chimed in, "On what? How do you figure that?"

"Well, little lady, the fence is going to need to be replaced for one thing."

Okay, they didn't really say little lady, but their eyes said it.

I told them, "This house was built in 2006, the fence isn't even five years old. The fence at my house is 14 years old and they just propped it up and put a few posts in it and it's fine."

They sat there and chuckled at me like I didn't know the difference between a two by four and a toilet.

"No, that's just ONE of the things that need to be done with that backyard," said Superintendent Moron.

His face was starting to turn from ballerina pink to a light fuchsia, which was how you could tell he was getting annoyed. My wimpy ass partner was squirming in his seat.

*Wow*, I thought, *what do these guys have on him that he's afraid of them?*

They went on to tell me that they were going to put concrete patios all over the backyard. I tried to explain to them that what made sense was to finish up the backyard with sod and bark and clean up the pool. By doing this, a potential buyer would be able to see a finished yard and not a bunch of weeds. This would be a yard someone could move into and use while they decided what improvements they wanted to do of their own, depending on their needs and tastes. I said this in the most eloquent way I could.

The room went silent. My husband, who knows me, had a look of, "Oh shit, now what's going to happen?" My partner looked like he wanted to hide under his desk. Superintendent Moron and No Ass Guy looked at me like Scooby Doo when he cocks his head to one side because he doesn't understand something. Then their faces turned into, "Why do we have this dumb female here and who brought her to the party?" They weren't buying it and they made no bones about it.

So, we went on to the interior of the house. Superintendent Moron wanted, or insisted on, painting the whole entire house to a tune of $7,000. That price may have been what you'd pay in 2005, but in this current economy, no one, including contractors, painters, real estate agents, or anything in between, are making what they once commanded for services. We would have been able to have that house painted for $4,000 or less by the painters I used.

But the house didn't even need painting. Superintendent Moron disagreed, saying that there were cracks in the house, so we should just paint the whole house to the tune of $7K. Why not fix the cracks and touch up the paint? There were several cans in the garage. We couldn't agree on this one and I couldn't let it go on principal, so we agreed that we would meet at the house with Kiss Ass Real Estate Agent, who was selling all our houses, to get his opinion as well.

The real estate agent we were using was someone I had handpicked. He used to be a loan officer and, like so many loan officers who wanted to jump onto the band wagon of something they thought would be easier than doing loans, he got into real estate. Shortly after he did, even though I've been a real estate agent for many years, I realized I couldn't do it all. Looking at the houses and going to the auction was a full plate, especially if I was going to need energy to fight with Superintendent Moron on every house, so I asked him to work with us. I gave him his first listing and taught him what to say. Too bad my ex partner is taking half his commision.

Working with real estate agents in our area requires strategy. You can't be too hard on them, or too tricky, because they don't get it and you'll scare them away. This real estate agent used to be a used car salesperson and he looks and acts just like one. He's short and stout; that's a nice way of saying he hasn't missed many meals. He drinks like a fish and smokes like a chimney. He's got a voice that sounds just like John Candy, the late comedian. He's a really fast talker, which I actually like, because you can get in a long conversation with him in a short period of time. I've met someone since then who used to be in the car business, too, and she's a real kiss ass as well. Maybe they take the "customer is always right" theory really seriously.

Kiss Ass Real Estate Agent is the type of guy who just moves from opportunity to opportunity, moving his lips to the next ass that benefits him.

I thought his "anything you want, I'm here for you with my mouth on your ass" kind of attitude would help me with Superintendent Moron, so we agreed to meet there later that day.

When I got to the house, Superintendent Moron and Kiss Ass were already there eyeing the interior, which looked better than I originally thought. Kiss Ass said that since he was paid no matter what we did to the house, it was in his best interest to do as much as we could to the house, so whatever we wanted to do would be fine. Arrrrgggggghhhh. Whose ass was he kissing now? I could see I was going to be on my own trying to convince Superintendent Moron.

In the end, I gave up and said, "Do whatever you want."

I was working with a bunch of idiots. Who, in their right mind, would argue with a woman who didn't want to spend all the money? Unless someone was on the take or someone wanted to bring in a bunch of money to their own construction company, because they made money on that, too. I'm just saying.

Halfway through this construction fix up, my partner must have started to get the invoices on that and other houses on which Superintendent Moron spent money like a drunken sailor. Knowing that my partner was the type who liked to pull up the rug and sweep everything under it, I realized it must have taken every ounce of gall he had to finally fire Superintendent Moron from the fix up of these houses. He was a partner with him in his construction company as well, so he couldn't get rid of him altogether, but at least he was out of my hair.

My partner had me step in because, not only was he too lazy, but he had moved over two and a half hours away, which is really a smart move if you're trying to run a hands-on business.

So I took over the fix up on that house. I got the concrete guy to let us out of a $22,000 contract for sidewalks and walkways all over the backyard and do it for $7,000. I tried to talk to the landscaper and see how much I could do with that bill, but he wouldn't budge much. Superintendent Moron had already approved an $18,000 bid for the sod in the front and back yards and the landscaper had his eye on a trip for his family to Mexico.

To show you how ridiculous this was, similar projects I've worked on since have been done for $4,000 or less.

To add insult to injury, when I went to the house to talk to the landscaper, he and his guys were in the back yard, propping up the posts and repairing a few of the boards on the fence. I asked in disbelief why they weren't putting up a new fence instead of just repairing everything.

"Your fence is older than this and we just repaired it," he smiled with these false pearly whites.

I stood there in the back yard with my fancy Macy's shoes covered in mud and dirt. Now it was me wearing the Scooby Doo face with my head cocked to one side, staring at him.

In the end, I bought that house with over $100,000 of equity. Based on previous houses and hundreds since, we should have made around $80,000 after my partner bilked his investors out of his bullshit fees and repairs, but by the time those guys butchered that remodel, we ended up losing money on the house.

My partner and I had worked out a deal where I got an acquisition fee for doing all the work involved with buying the house at the courthouse steps. When the house closed, he took that fee away from me because he said that we didn't make any money on that house and it was a team effort, so since I was part of that team, I had to give up my share.

"Are you *blankety blank* kidding me?" I asked him.

I was the one who tried to stop the hemorrhaging of spending on that house and he had fired Superintendent Moron halfway through. I probably saved over $30,000 in costs and he was taking my piddley ass fee away? I should have known then to walk away, but I stayed to take more abuse. That was just the beginning.

Once Superintendent Moron was gone, nobody really stepped in to supervise the construction crew. Can you imagine anything more stupid than turning over a house to guys who are getting paid by the hour with no one in charge and basically giving them carte blanche, including credit cards to the home stores, and relying on them to fix up the houses in a timely manner? I will probably never know the extent of the embezzlement style of my then partner, but suffice it to say, he moved away shortly after we started buying houses together, so he wasn't around to crack the whip and didn't seem to care how many hours they charged on a house. You've got to ask yourself, why? I can only assume what he was rigging because he was in charge of the books and to this day I haven't seen any reconciling, except what he manufactured when I insisted.

Having these guys work on the houses was like having a bunch of teenagers working with us. They were about as reliable and just as evasive. I developed a look for almost every house that included the same color palette to make it easy for the subcontractors. It was more convenient and quicker for us because we didn't have to spend time trying to pick colors or patterns for each house. If we were going to need new linoleum, there was a standard pattern we used. If we used tile, whatever was the least expensive at the home store was what we bought. The carpet, landscaping, light fixtures and accessories were almost always the same. The extent of the fix up depended on the price of the house and the location.

But these construction guys, not being accountable for anything, took it upon themselves to do or not do whatever they wanted in the houses they were working on. This became a source of contention because they weren't privy to the price we paid for the house or how much we intended to list it for.

After months and months of doing houses and then screwing up on every one by over or under fixing, we decided I would go through the house when we got it and make a detailed list of what needed to be done. I would type out this list and put it on the front door, so if different guys were working on the house, they would know what needed to be done.

It seemed so simple to me and such a good way to keep the fix up costs in check. I'm sure when I left they flipped me off as I exited the room, but I didn't care. I didn't have time to run after people to get things done. My partner thought it was a great idea, too. Yeah, as long as he didn't have to do anything. The system would have worked if they had actually stuck to the list, but they knew that they would never have to be accountable to anyone, especially my partner because he never reined them in at all or spoke to them about the costs.

After chasing them around for over two years, everything finally came to a head when I was supposed to be going away for the weekend. Instead, I spent my Saturday going from house to house and seeing all the extra items these guys were doing in these ghetto houses, like taking the time and money to rip out a ceiling and put in can lights, pulling out perfectly good carpet and ruining brand new carpet because they were tracking in mud. The list goes on and on.

After I split with them, I learned so much from the subcontractors. The painters informed me that the construction crew members told them that they were padding all the bills, charging for eight hours and really only working two or three hours on a house. They said that they knew which houses to do that on because someone was telling them. Gee, I wonder who that was. Probably the same guy who was duping his investors by giving them a lot of double talk. I had a suspicion about it while we were working together, but I figured it didn't really have anything to do with me because, after all, they weren't my investors, even though I seemed to be the only one who was trying to save them money and had their best interest in mind.

They've gone on to continue in the flipping business and we're actually in competition, vying for the same houses at the courthouse steps. Since then, I've seen them buy a house with an IRS lien on it, which meant they were stuck with it for four months before they could sell it, a house with $30,000 in back taxes that they obviously didn't know because that would have wiped out almost all of the equity and houses that were so bad they would have been condemned if the city came around and inspected them.

But, they keep going; after all it's only money. And it's obviously easier when it's someone else's.

## Chapter 7

# LOOKING AT HOUSES

When I was a real estate agent, I can remember driving down the street and seeing out of the corner of my eye a house I thought was vacant. I'd reverse my car, get the address and start my research on how to find the owner, and how to contact them to see if I could list the house for sale. We didn't even have computers then, or the internet. I know I sound old, but too bad. We had to be more resourceful, so we were better, ha, ha. I did all kinds of crazy crap, like talking to neighbors, looking in the mailbox, searching through old MLS books. Wow, I forgot about that until now.

We used to get a book delivered to our offices for the week that would have all the current listings. The pages were like newspaper newsprint and the covers were different colors every week and alternated between a bright blue, green, gold and pink, and I remember some pukey baby poop brown color that was like my Century 21 jacket.

My husband calls it house sense. I had it then and I think I still have it now. Wandering through the streets, when I look at a house that's coming up for a trustee sale, most of the time I can tell if the house is vacant or not. The tell tale signs are notices posted on the front door, an open side gate, blinds all closed up, nothing on the porch, like chairs or plants. No mail in the mailbox is another good sign that no one is currently living in the house because the post office usually stops delivering mail once they know that a house is vacant. Sometimes they'll even put a big rubber band on a mailbox so all the postmen will know not to deliver any mail.

Often the lawn is dead and it's obvious it's vacant, but other times the lawn is manicured and green, especially with the mild California winters. We bought a home in a beautiful neighborhood, one of the nicest in the city. When I drove by, it looked like someone still lived there. The lawn was great and the house had an enormous amount of curb appeal. I've gotten a lot braver since then, but at that time, I didn't want to put my fat head up to the front door or windows in case someone happened to be walking by inside the house.

I always scope the street for neighbors, which, so far, have never steered me wrong. A guy was working in his garage down the street and I asked him if that house was vacant. He told me the people had moved out and lived in the area, so they kept a gardener working on the lawn, and they kept the water on to maintain the landscaping.

I ended up bidding against a few other people and I got the house. The neighbor was right. It was beautiful inside and had all the stainless steel appliances intact. The carpet, walls, trim and everything was beautiful. I paid $425,000 at the auction and sold it for $600,000. The only things I did were landscape the backyard, drain and clean the pool, and touch up the paint inside.

You always have to be thinking in this real estate flipping business. If these people cared enough about a house they were losing to still maintain the landscaping, then it would stand to reason that the inside would be nicely maintained as well.

Anyone can look at a house that has a dead lawn, papers piled up on the driveway and weeds up the kazoo and figure out that the house is vacant. But to really get the upper hand, you need to do a little bit of homework.

Talking to neighbors is a great start. If I can't find any, I'll try the water. If that's off, there's a very good chance that no one is living there. I say good chance and not for sure because there are always exceptions to the rule, which I'll get to later. You can go right up to the door and if you hear the beeping of a smoke detector, it's probably vacant. Who can live with that racket going on 24/7?

But lately, since there's more competition, people from the courthouse or their partners are trying to get trickier. I always have one ear on conversations going on around me. That's one of the reasons I started bringing crocheting in a bag to the steps. That and because I was bored in between the breaks, not to mention standing around waiting for my house or houses to come up for auction. So, I started making scarves for a homeless shelter in San Francisco called Glide Memorial Church.

Remember that movie with Will Smith called "The Pursuit of Happyness?" The main character and his son went and stayed at that shelter. I figured it was a good thing to do. It would cure my boredom and it's always cold in San Francisco, especially if you have to sleep out in the streets. Not only does it hopefully bring up the good karma factor, but I stand there totally engrossed in my crocheting and no one really notices that I'm listening to every word they say.

I remember one of my first buys there. I had been there for a couple of weeks checking it out and then I came with about a million dollars in my purse. Don't get too excited, it was cashier's checks, not cold hard cash. I was bidding like crazy on a house and some guy was on the phone with his apparent investor.

He said frantically, "I don't know, it's some lady who's knitting." The person on the other end must have said, "What the hell did you say?" He repeated, "She's knitting... yeah, and bidding. No, knitting like with yarn."

It was all I could do to keep a straight face.

Armed with my crocheting, I hear guys telling each other all the time how they try to fool everyone by putting old shoes on the porch, or items that will make people think the house is occupied. Of course, not to be outdone, another will say how he not only puts out shoes, but he carries patio furniture in his truck to put in front of houses.

I mean, come on, men. I'm really going to try not to sound like a man basher right now, but any women reading this will shake their heads and think, *Why in the heck would you tell anyone what you're doing to try and trick people? Especially, the very people you're trying to trick!*

One time, I found a house I wanted to buy. It had been listed in the past, so there was a real estate agent lockbox still on the front door. I used my MLS key to open the lockbox, but there was no key inside. I chalked it up to the fact that the old listing agent probably either came and got it to give back to someone, or it just got misplaced during the listing period, which is common.

I ended up buying the house and the guy who I was bidding against told me after I had won that he had the key to the house in his truck! He was the one who went and looked all through the house and then took the key. I cracked up laughing to myself because this was one of the good guys. I guess he wanted to prevent anyone from looking at the house in detail so they wouldn't bid as much as he did. Obviously, it backfired. "Why does she keep talking about good guys and bad guys?" you say. You've got to stay tuned because it will become very clear later why I've separated them into two groups.

One of the funniest stories about someone trying to trick people is this one. I saw this house coming up the next day when I was looking at the foreclosure website. Usually, when a house comes up with a minimum bid that late, like the night before, it means it probably will sell and not postpone to a later date, which many of them do.

It was probably ten o'clock at night, but the house was a really good one and about a mile from my house, so I asked my husband if he wanted to take a look. We headed over there and all the lights were out. Not that unusual for those kinds of freaky people who get up at six o'clock in the morning, so that didn't confirm anything.

There was a white truck in the driveway. That's not a deal killer, either, because often neighbors park in the driveways of foreclosure homes when their garages are full. The lawn was pretty good; even though it was dark, I could make that out. We couldn't tell if the house was occupied or not, and since it was nighttime, we couldn't ask any neighbors, so we went home.

The next day while waiting for the auction, I was sitting at a nearby Starbucks. My husband had gone by the house in the daytime and he still couldn't figure it out. Suddenly a light bulb went off in my head. I called the local utility company and told them that I was buying this house. Hey, I was planning on buying it. I was concerned that there might be issues with the utilities, so could they tell me if the power was on.

"No ma'am, the power is turned off on that house," the unsuspecting utility customer service person told me.

Ha, ha. Okay. Now I was in the game. The auction went on that day and I ended up bidding against another local real estate agent and his partner. I got the house and after the auction, I called my locksmith to meet me there to open it up because it was one of those houses that was all closed up and I really wanted to get in and see the inside.

When I arrived at the house, the truck was still there. Mmmm. So if it was a neighbor's truck, they never went to work that day, because it was early afternoon. One of the neighbors came over to see what the heck we were doing breaking into this house and I told him the circumstances. This guy was like the unofficial neighborhood watch. I asked him if that truck was his.

"No," he said, shaking his head.

"Is it familiar to you?" I asked.

"No," he added, but he went on to tell me that the night before, about 9:30p.m., a couple of guys came in two different trucks. One guy parked the truck in the driveway and then got into the other truck, and they both left, leaving the first truck in the driveway.

"Really? What did these guys look like?" I asked him, starting to get the picture.

"Well, they were two white guys about 40 to 50 in age." He was now enthused that something exciting was finally happening in the neighborhood.

Okay, I figured it had to be someone from the courthouse steps. That description covers basically everyone who is there, except the young kids in their late 20s or early 30s. I chuckled to myself because my plan was that I was going to teach them a lesson for trying to get one over on everyone.

I called the local police department. No, since the car was in a driveway, they considered it private property. That's good scoop if you're ever in this position. Get ten of your closest friends and lift the car onto the street. You think it can't be done? Side story here.

Many years ago, I went and visited my best friend from high school in Santa Rosa, California at the college she was going to. We went to a wild party one night and my car was parked on the street outside her dorm.

When we woke up the next morning, someone said,

"Did you see what the football team did to that car outside?"

Ha, ha, ha, ha.

*Oh shit,* I thought. My car was parked outside. They had picked up my whole car and put it on a neighbor's lawn down the street. Apparently, they really needed a parking space. So, it can be done.

The police told me that since it was on private property, they couldn't tow it, but they asked for the license plate number. It seems there is a caveat to this private property thing, which is, if the vehicle is stolen, they can come and get it. I read off the plate. Shoot. Not stolen. Okay. Now what? They told me I could call a tow company and pay to have it towed.

*Yeah, that works,* I thought. *I'll pay, I don't care.*

I was getting a kick out of this and the locksmith was just shaking his head, snickering while watching me go through this as I paced the driveway.

I was on the phone with the towing company, describing my ordeal and asking them to come right away when all of a sudden, two guys roll up in a truck. I looked closer and it was the guy who was bidding against me and his partner. We all started laughing hysterically when they pulled up. I hung up with the tow company and told them who I was on the phone with.

The one I was bidding against said, "I told my buddy we had to get back to the truck. She'll tow it."

He said his buddy disagreed, "No, she won't do that."

The bidder said, "You don't know her. She will."

And we were cracking up, knowing he was right. He said they had stopped at Costco and he told his buddy they had to go because I'll tow his truck away. He thought for sure he had outsmarted anyone who would have been bidding against him. NOT.

I must confess here that I'm not totally innocent in this tricking thing, but at least my tricks are way more convincing.

My husband and I looked at a house that was going to be sold the next day. It was a great house. The lawn was fine, but it was all closed up, so we really thought it was occupied. I saw someone down the street working on their car and I went over to talk to him. He said that the house was indeed vacant, but the neighbors kept up the lawn because they didn't want the neighborhood to look bad. Ah ha.

We really liked that house and wanted to get it. It was around Christmas time and everyone had their lights or decorations on but this house. I had an idea. We went to the dollar store in town and got a wreath for the door and some candy cane decorations for the lawn. We came back after dark and put everything in our arsenal in its place. We stepped back and admired our handy work and laughed and laughed. Well, really quietly because we didn't want to arouse any neighbors. The house totally looked occupied. I mean, who would have fresh decorations if they weren't living there?

The next day the house came up for auction with a minimum bid that was too high for anyone to bid on and it went back to the bank, decorations and all.

Sometimes in this business, it's better not to talk to the neighbors. I had purchased a property with a guy who was this prim and proper type from a San Francisco skyscraper office. We were in a lovely part of the ghetto. I mean we paid $65,000 for the house, what did we expect? He was asking me all kinds of questions as far as what we were going to do in terms of renovating the house. We went outside and noticed the neighbor was out there with his young daughter.

My investor approached the guy and, with as proper an English accent as you can imagine, said, "Tell me, how is the neighborhood?"

I mean, shit, as if he couldn't tell by the gangbangers driving by with tunes blasting from their radios like, "I'm gonna kill you, bitch."

The neighbor proceeded to tell him with a straight face, "Well, we did have a meth lab a few doors down, but they've been gone for a few months now because the police busted them up, and there was a drive by shooting over there on that corner last week, and kids like to come right here and spin doughnuts with their cars in the middle of the night, which wakes us up, but aside from that, it's pretty good."

Are you freaking kidding me? Aside from that? And he was serious! I was pissing myself and wanted to get back in the house, but the investor didn't seem that startled. Based on that lovely image the neighbor presented, I suggested we do a spit and polish on that house and move on before we needed to go to the emergency room.

We didn't spend very much to get it to sale and we ended up selling it for $109,000. Not too shabby for a couple of months' work.

I drove by that house about a year later and whoever bought it had painted it, given it a new front door and redone the landscaping and it looked like a million bucks... well, a million bucks surrounded by dollar store houses.

You never know what you'll find in some of these questionable neighborhoods. I bought a house that looked good enough from the outside. Once we got in and I started going through the house with the locksmith, we found scaffolding in all the bedrooms. I really couldn't figure out why in the heck they would have that in all their bedrooms.

"Were these circus performers, or was this a business where they trained construction guys to stand on scaffolding?" I looked at the locksmith.

Of course I was kidding about the training part, but what about the acrobatics? He reached onto one of the plywood shelves and pulled up a lovely leaf that looked like a pretty seven point star.

"Oh," was all I had to say.

They weren't circus people. They were growing pot.

But it's not always the ghetto where all the crap

happens. Someone I know from the auction was telling me they had a house that was closing escrow on a Monday. It was in a very nice neighborhood where the houses were over $500,000. On Friday, a van pulled up and someone broke in and stole all the appliances. She showed me photos of how beautiful the house looked with those sparkling new stainless steel appliances and then what it looked like with holes in the walls where the double oven, microwave, dishwasher, and cook top used to be.

She said she knew it was a white van because the neighbors said they had seen it in the middle of the day. They didn't think anything of it because there had been people working on the house for the past few weeks. I told her that sucked, but at least the house was still standing. That's me, always seeing the positive.

One time when I bought a house in that same neighborhood, I was bidding against someone who shall remain nameless, you know, like they say in Harry Potter about Voldemort. I went and looked inside the windows in the morning. Everything looked good. All the cabinets were there, even though the appliances were gone, and even though it seemed a little dirty, it was in pretty good shape.

I came back to the house after I bought it in the afternoon. It looked like a bomb went off inside. There were holes all over the walls in almost every room except the front, of course, where someone would have been able to see what was happening. It seemed like someone took a hammer and went through the whole house with it. The cabinet doors had been ripped off the hinges and even the freaking circular staircase had been pulled down and was hanging off the stairs, ready to fall like in a bad horror movie.

I had placed insurance on the property the moment I got it, so most of the cost was covered. That was one of the first houses I ever bought and I almost think it was a message from someone to get off those steps. Like when they send you a dead canary or something like that and leave it on your doorstep.

Another time we went to this house in a great area to see what kind of condition it was in because it was coming up for auction. Like so many, it was all closed up, but there was a gate, which was locked.

Often times, banks hire field workers to go out and inspect properties that have notice of defaults filed on them. If the house is vacant, they'll put a lock on the gate to the backyard and close it up. Then, somehow, if it has a pool, the vector control is called to monitor the pool. I don't think they come back over and over, but instead, they go to the pool and put these little mosquito eating fish in because they're concerned about West Nile virus. Once they do that, they put a red stop sign on the fence with a big sign that says there's a pool there and there are fish in it eating the bugs. The fish are so tiny, you can barely see them. They're sort of like guppies, very unassuming little black fish. By the time the vector control gets there to implement this practice, the pool is green, so you can't see the fish very well anyway. I have bought many houses where the pools look like they have green pudding in them. Yum.

So, this house had the stop sign and a wood fence that was probably eight or nine feet high. It's a good thing my husband is thin and very athletic. He jumped over that fence like he was in the Olympics. Of course, I would never be able to get my fat butt over it, so I had to wait impatiently to get his evaluation.

Apparently, the house seemed vacant, although there was still a lot of stuff left behind. Many of the properties are like this, though. It's non descriptive stuff. You could fill up a whole truck with these items, like a black garbage bag filled with old clothes, some shoes, candlesticks, old papers, bedding. Nothing big that you can really describe, so I didn't think anything of that.

It did, in fact, have a pool; a pudding pool. It backed up to the golf course and had a great back yard. The air conditioner was there and so was all the pool equipment. That's really important because those are some big ticket items. The air conditioner you could negotiate and deal with, but the pool equipment is expensive. If that's missing, and so many houses that are foreclosed on are missing it, it will cost you thousands.

It came up for auction a couple of days later and there were only a couple of bidders, and I ended up getting it.

One of the guys who was there said, "I would have gone for that house, but I just couldn't get over the fence."

"Oh, yeah," I agreed, "Me either. I'm just going to take a chance."

I realized after a few of these episodes that I missed my calling as an actress.

After we purchased that house and the pool people came to start cleaning up the pudding, they let me know that they found a hawk, an opossum, a raccoon and several rats in the pool. It was on a golf course and so many of those critters frequent those kinds of places. They were probably strolling around the course and thought they'd have a little drink in this big pond.

But that's not the most interesting pool story. We bought a house once with a pudding pool that had three full size mattresses in it. When the pool guys called me up to tell me they were done draining the pool and that they found three mattresses in it, I thought I hadn't heard them correctly. Can you imagine how pissed the previous homeowners must have been to hurl those mattresses into that pool?

Sometimes, if I go and look at a house and the gate is locked, I'll call my husband, who is 50, but in really good shape. He's an avid bicyclist who runs and works out and is so proud of himself that he's 50 and can still scale an eight foot fence.

I'm really impressed by this behavior because of my firsthand experience. I went by a house that was up for auction the next day, but my husband wasn't available. I was able to put some garbage cans close to the fence, though, and get over to the other side so I could see the back yard and the kitchen. But in my haste, I didn't really think about how I was going to get back over to the other side. There wasn't anything to put next to the fence to climb back over.

Somehow, stepping on parts of the fence, I managed to get my butt up and on top of the fence. Once I was there, I didn't realize how high that fence was from the ground. Here I was, sitting on top of this fence that was about eight feet high, with a dress on and high heel shoes. I was twisting and turning, trying to figure out what I was going to do and somehow my dress slipped up and managed to get caught on the fence post, and I ripped my underwear. I must have been a spectacle. I'm so glad I didn't see anyone watching me. Oh shit, knowing me I would have waved.

I took off my shoes and threw them down on the ground. I didn't know how I was going to get off of that fence, especially since the gate was now holding my underwear hostage with my butt attached. But I knew I wasn't going to be able to do it in heels. I worked up the courage to jump onto the cement, fell on my shoulder and kind of rolled to a stop. I was a little battered, but fine. That was the last fence I jumped.

Recently, I was in a nicer area looking at houses coming up for auction for the week. I drove past the house I wanted to look at and I just got the feeling that it was vacant. It was all closed up, but the sun was really bright and sometimes in this heat people will close up the house until it cools down. The lawn was green and manicured, but I couldn't shake that feeling that I thought it was empty.

I parked my car across the street and down a few houses. I could see that the wood blinds were covering all the windows except for one close to the front door that had an opening on the bottom about an inch where you could see inside. I walked up to the front porch and pretended like I was ringing the doorbell in case any snoopy neighbors were watching. I didn't want anyone giving me the third degree about why I was on their front porch. I just wanted to get my head close to that one inch gap.

So, I stood there for a few seconds and casually looked through that gap. Ah ha. It was vacant.

"I knew it," I said, talking to myself. "Yeah, you go girl." I like to answer myself, too.

I was meandering around on the porch when a car drove up and stopped in the middle of the street. A younger girl rolled down her window and smiled.

"Are you doing the same thing I am?" she said cunningly.

"No," I said, and looked at her with a "what the heck are you talking about?" kind of stare.

"Oh," she stuttered.

Hee, hee, she thought she was busted by the homeowner. This was someone who was either interested in buying the house at the auction, or working for someone who was going to bid.

"Are you Megan?" she questioned.

"Yeah," I said with a completely straight face, not knowing who this Megan was, but assuming it was the homeowner.

"Oh, so you're still living in the house?" she went on.

"Yeah," I said with my best valley girl attitude.

I hadn't thought about what would happen next if she questioned me further. She was getting nervous now and I was kind of enjoying it.

"Well, I work for Joe Blow and the Joe Blow Group. I'll just tell them the house is occupied," she said nervously.

"Yeah," I said.

I actually was taking on an attitude with her. I mean,

who was she to come and try to buy the house I was living in? See, when I perform, I really get into character. She drove away and I was chuffed with myself, as the English say, knowing that I had gotten one over on Joe Blow and his group, who are one of my main competitors.

Once in a while now, I'll go up to the door of a house that's coming up for auction and there will be some half assed sign on the door saying, "I'm renting the house, don't buy it," or something lame like that. Obviously put up by another bidder trying to scare competition away.

I looked at a house where the lawn was dead and there were no blinds on the freaking eight foot wide window, or any other windows for that matter. You could see straight through the entire house, which was completely vacant without one item left behind. There was a sign made of copy paper next to the doorbell that said, "Please don't disturb tenants." Ha, ha, ha. What were they miniature tenants who were exhibitionists? Amateurs. You'll have to get up a lot earlier in the morning than that to fool me. I bought the house the next day at the auction.

You might be asking, "Why are these people going through such great lengths to trick others into thinking the house is occupied?" A few reasons. If a house is occupied, it's going to probably cost you to help the occupants to move. In the beginning, people were so excited at the prospect of getting a few thousand dollars to move, but now that this whole cash for keys thing is mainstream, they've become a lot more demanding. Even the banks offer cash for keys.

Plus, there are different rules for tenants and owners. You can make educated guesses as to if a house is occupied by either, but there is no surefire way unless you talk to whoever is living there. Most of the time, someone who is living in a house and is the owner has been bugged so much by people knocking on their door and calling them that they're sick of being bothered. If it's tenants, chances are, they're working to pay the rent, so they don't answer.

Tenants currently have the right to stay in the property through their lease term. I discuss this in further detail in the tenants chapter, but basically they rented the property in good faith. Usually, they continue to make their rent payments even though an owner isn't paying the mortgage. It really isn't the tenants' fault, so legislature was passed in the last year to protect renters from having to move over and over again because houses are being foreclosed out from under them.

The other crappy thing about this is that tenants have

to give a first and last month's rent and deposit, or some combination of that. I have never heard of a poor tenant who got their deposit back from the old owner. In fact, we bought a house in town that had a tenant who was a single mom putting her son through college. She wasn't even paying the market rate, but we wanted to give her a break, so she stayed in the property and continued paying her same rental amount. A few days after we bought it at the auction, the previous homeowner came back and wanted to take the appliances out of the house like the stove, dishwasher and microwave. She called us because she didn't know what to do. The guy told her that he was entitled to take those out of the house. On what planet, dude? We told her not to let him in and we'd tell him why.

When I first started looking at houses before they came up for auction, I would tell the neighbors that the house was coming up for a trustee sale. I would ask if it was vacant or what the house was like, how long the people had been out and so forth. I've found people in any neighborhood are happy to tell you all of their neighbor's dirty laundry. Things I don't even care about knowing. But I always stand there politely and nod and comment on their story. Hey, my mom raised me right.

I'd see a house come up the next week on the same street and the house up for auction would be the neighbor I had spoken to the week before. At least I knew it was occupied! But it made me think about my original rap. So, after a while, I started saying that I was a real estate agent, which was true, and that the house was coming up for sale. I didn't mention the fact that it was a trustee sale; it was still a sale.

Sometimes neighbors are savvy and know it's a trustee sale. It's funny because they use lingo that clues me in to the fact that they know what's going on, but they won't really come out and say it. I think they're sparing me any gruesome details. Little do they know. I just play dumb, which I'm very good at and comfortable with.

Looking at these houses can become a scary thing, especially in some of the neighborhoods I venture into. I've had some small scares, but there are a few that stand out in my mind.

I was in an area that isn't the worst around, but I certainly wouldn't go for a walk there by myself at night. There was a house coming up for auction and before I went to look at it, I saw it on the MLS as active, meaning it was for sale. On these profiles, they always give the status of the occupancy so real estate agents know how to go about showing the property without disturbing anyone. The profile said it was vacant and no advance notice was necessary to look at the house.

I drove down the street, canvassing the houses, looking for the house number I was searching for. It was halfway down the street on the right side. I took a good look and realized that there were no blinds on the front window, or they must have been open, because it seemed like you could see right into the house.

So, I stopped my car and parked in front of the house. Usually I like to be a little slyer and park a few houses down, but this house apparently was vacant and there supposedly was a lockbox for real estate agents to get in. I went right up to the house and looked on the front door for the lockbox. They usually put them on the doorknob when the property is vacant, but there was nothing there.

I stepped over a flower box, put my hands on the window and peeked in. Well, more like I put my whole face on the window and scoured the inside with my eyes. Yep, it was certainly vacant. There wasn't a thing inside that I could see. It was unusual that I could see right through to the kitchen. I could see that it had white tile countertops and the appliances were still there. I liked what I saw, especially since it had an opening bid of

$87,000 and it was worth about $149,000.

I thought I'd go over to the side and see if the listing agent put the lockbox on the water pipe or the utilities meter. There was a side gate, but no meters in front of it, so I opened the gate to the back yard. As I opened it, the side door from the garage closed. My heart skipped a beat. Mmmm, that was weird. It could have closed from the wind. I looked closer and it hadn't closed completely; it was now ajar. I was still at the side gate, obviously too chicken to get any closer.

I backed up without even looking behind me and latched the gate. As I started to walk to the front of the house, I could hear some kind of scuffling. I could tell there was something going on around that house, but I couldn't figure out if it was in the back yard or the side, or even inside the house.

Now I was spooked, so I shuffled over to the front sidewalk and waited for something to happen. I wasn't sure what I was waiting for, but I somehow thought maybe I'd see someone running out of the house. I didn't really think far enough ahead about what I would do if someone really did come out, because I was in a little bit of shock, I think. I probably would have pooped my pants if someone rushed out of the house, but I didn't think about it at that moment.

I decided to get in my car and just go with the information I had already collected. I headed down the street to where it ended. I turned my car around and started to make another pass by the house. When I drove by and looked at the front, the blinds were no longer open; someone had been in the house and closed them! This might not seem like a big deal to you, sitting there reading this book in your PJs, but when it says on the MLS that the house is vacant, then the house is vacant. This is the go ahead for real estate agents to get the key and go in unannounced.

It turns out, as I was leaving to get into my car after the garage door closed, I saw the lockbox, which had been hidden when the flowers in front of it grew right up over it. What freaked me out was that the house was supposed to be vacant, so there was no way I was going in now. In this area, because of the incredibly large amount of foreclosures, I've heard so many stories of squatters moving into houses and I wasn't waiting around to find out if this was one of those instances.

Although freaked out that someone had broken or moved in, I got the house at the auction the next day. Once I bought the property, I sure as hell wasn't going to go inside. I called the locksmith to open up the house and see if he had to chase anyone out.

I've often overheard one of our competitors talking about how they'd break into houses so they could get the full scoop on the condition of the house before they bid. Thinking back, it could have been one of their guys checking out the house and closing the blinds. In the end, no one was in the house, but every time I had to go there to take a look at the renovation, I wouldn't go alone.

I'm not sure if that is the most frightening, or if this next episode is. Let me preface this by saying that I am a big chicken when it comes to criminals and crime in general. I read the paper every day and I sometimes sleep with one eye open if I hear a noise that goes bump in the night. I'll get fixated on a crime that's committed when it's reported in the paper and I'll read all the follow up trial reports. Hey, it's my own little town CSI I have going on here. I'm fascinated by these criminals. Maybe this is why I hung around the criminals at the courthouse steps for so long. Wait until you get to that chapter.

The stupid thing is that I live in a town where nothing really bad ever happens. If you read those crime logs in the paper (which I do), they're funny because they report things like someone's bike was stolen or someone was walking down the street, found to be intoxicated and hauled off. Anyway, there was this guy who I shall call Leslie Vinton. Okay, that wasn't his real name, but I'm sure he would come looking for me if I used his real name, so no way you'll get it out of me. Here's why.

This guy was some kind of serial rapist dude. Well, not kind of, he was. I've lived in the area for over 20 years, so I remember when they caught him and put him away. He apparently was in jail for quite some time and was finally to be released. The big story and controversy was where they were going to put this guy once he got out of jail. I think he might have gone to a group home for a short period of time and when he was to be let out on his own, so to speak, they were going to do it close to the area I live in. It's about 10 miles from my house and where I look at all these houses coming up for auction.

So here I am, la, la, la, la, going on my merry way in the next town, looking at houses I might be interested in. I drove around the corner of a street and stopped in front of the address of the house I had on my list. I went up to the window and looked in because I could tell it was vacant. There were a few pieces of furniture there, but they looked like the kind of pieces someone would have left behind. So I turned around and started to go back to my car.

As I made my way closer, I glanced across the street and down a bit to see a man coming out of his house. As my daughters would say, he did look a bit ghetto, but the house he came out of was very nice. It had a lovely dark beige color paint job with a dark red door, and the lawn and front yard were very well maintained.

"Hi," I said, looking his way.

"Hi," he said in an ever-so-friendly voice.

He started to cross the street. I strolled over to him and we met halfway in the middle of the street. It was a very lonely neighborhood, so there were no cars on the road.

I swear, the next few words out of his mouth sounded like, "Blue map folder, gate jeans, cup."

It was pretty much that incoherent. I raised my eyebrow to try and figure out what the heck this guy was saying.

"Uh, I'm looking at this house because it's coming up for sale," I said, trying to get a hold of the conversation.

"Oh is it?" he questioned. This I understood.

"Yeah, it seems pretty nice," I said. "But your house is really nice. And what a beautiful front yard you have," I added.

"Oh, this ain't my house," he groaned. Oh my God, was it better or worse that I could understand him a little better now? "No, no, I'm going off to a group supervised home," he said nonchalantly. Just after he said that, he put out his hand and said, "By the way, nice to meet you, baby. My name is Leslie."

I reached out my hand and looked at his face... oh shit!!!!!! Leslie Vinton.

As he was sizing me up and licking his chops, I was thinking, *What is he looking at me like that for? I'm an old lady.*

I shook his hand and looked back at my car to see how far away it was. Now remember, there wasn't a soul around and this was a very quiet court. No one around to hear you scream. I had that scared feeling like when you can hear your heart beating in your ears. I just started nervously babbling and started backing up to get the blankity blank back to my car.

"Okay, it was nice meeting you. Nice to see you. Okay, then. Take it easy," was all I heard come out of my mouth.

"Where you goin' in such a hurry, baby?" He was looking me up and down.

I mean, really, I felt kind of fat that day. What was he thinking? Baby?

"Oh, I have to get back to work, ha, ha, ha." More nervous laughing and then I freaking moved my fat ass and feet back to my car so fast my head was spinning. I jumped in my car and locked the door behind me. Still trying to be cool, I actually turned and waved goodbye. He was still standing there in the middle of the street, checking me out. Oh, thank God I didn't put those license plates on my car and still had the paper ones from the dealer so there was no trace of me. That was what I got for reading the paper.

It's very rare that a neighbor gives incorrect information, but one time I was looking at a house that was coming up for auction. I stopped a few houses down and got out because it looked like it was vacant and I wanted to get a closer look. There was a nice couple next door to the house, working on their front yard.

I smiled and said, "This house is coming up for sale." I pointed to the house next door. "Do you know if it's vacant or not?"

With broken English, they told me, "Yes, yes."

Maybe I should have clued into the fact that they didn't really say anything but "yes, yes," but it was getting late and I was tired. I had been at the auction all day and I just wanted to look at this house, go home, eat and take off my pantyhose.

"Okay, thank you," I said with my kindest smile. "I'm just going to take a look at it."

They just smiled and smiled and nodded their heads.

*Gee, these people are nice,* I thought.

I went up to the front window of the house. It was a really large picture window about five feet wide. It was an older home in a bad area, so that larger type window was common. But this one had some kind of tinting on it or something and I couldn't see inside. I put my fat head right up to the window. Mmmm. I couldn't really see a thing. So, I planted my nostrils a little closer and tilted my head to get a better viewing point. All of a sudden, the door to the house swung open.

"Hey, muthaf**ker, what you doing, putting your head all up in my business?"

Well, first of all, I thought, *I can assure you I am no muthaf**ker*. And I don't think by business he meant his place of business establishment. To make it even scarier, there was a security type steel door in front of the one that he flung open, so I couldn't see a thing.

"Oh, hey, sorry man," I said. "Those neighbors told me that the house was vacant. I'm just trying to find my daughter a place to rent."

*God forgive me for lying*, I was thinking, *and don't let this gangsta kill me for it.*

The bummer was I still couldn't see his face, so I wouldn't be able to identify him if he popped a cap in me. That's gangsta talk for shooting up my ass. Oh, wait, the neighbors could.

*Okay, that's good*, I thought. Those thoughts must have been flying through my head like a carnival Tilt-A-Whirl.

"They stupid, they don't know nuttin'," he pronounced.

"Yeah, they are stupid," I agreed.

I was perfectly happy to bad mouth the neighbors who were so willing to help me a few minutes before. Hell, it was everyone for themselves here.

Still behind that steel door, he said, "They don't even know no English."

*Shit*, I thought. Those stupid asses nodding and telling me the house was vacant. Didn't they know there was a gangsta ready to kill me on the other side of that freaking steel door?

"Yeah, they told me this house was vacant. Can you believe that shit?" I said to him while casually backing off the porch.

I looked over at the neighbors and they were looking back at me and smiling and smiling. Right now I wanted to slap those smiles right off their faces, but I had to figure out a way to get off this porch and back into my car without being shot.

"Well, sorry man... Yeah, those stupid neighbors. What the blah, blah, blah?"

I just threw those neighbors so far under the bus because right now I had to save my own butt. He was talking and I was nervously talking at the same time backing up off the porch. I think in the end we were on the same page with neighbor bashing, but I can't be sure. My gangsta vocabulary only goes so far. I jumped into my car, managing to give the neighbors a dirty look while they smiled back at me. I never did see the face of the gangsta behind the door.

## Chapter 8

# DON'T MESS WITH A MOM

In my household, when we have a big story to tell, it starts out with "So," and a long pause combined with a look that implies you should be sitting down. Now this type of preface will be followed by a big story like somebody's pregnant, someone's divorcing, or something that is jaw dropping. It's a running joke in our house.

We'll come in and all one of us has to say is, "So..." and put hands down on the counter. We all stop and say, "Uh oh," or "Ew, let's hear it."

I write all of this because this next story is one of the big ones.

So...

I was at the steps for a property that I had looked at that morning. When I pulled up to check out the house, the first thing I saw was a huge piece of plywood over the entire front door and over the large picture frame window in the front of the house.

*Oh, no*, I thought as I pulled up, but aside from that, the house looked really good. I know, you're probably waiting for the punch line, but I'm serious, here. It did look good.

It wasn't long after I arrived at the courthouse that morning that the house came up for auction. I bid a penny over on the house and there were quite a few that followed my lead and bid $100 more each time. I was in the mindset that since there were so many others bidding on the property, it would go on for a while. It often does because, by qualifying, these guys usually have the intent of bidding a few times, at least before they stop. But not this time. I was getting my checks ready and someone asked me a question. I turned around for about 10 seconds to answer. In a fleeting 10 seconds, the auctioneer did his going once, going twice, sold to Jaime. Jaime threw his checks to the auctioneer and it was sold.

I turned around during this and said, "$100 more."

No, he bid and got the house, the auctioneer told me.

"What?" I questioned.

I could hear all those guys whispering and then they all let out a huge collective laugh. They were having a good joke at my expense.

What they do, and stay with me here, is they all bid, look around and see who is bidding. When they saw that it was all the usual crooks, and that I was distracted, they stopped because they all talked to each other about going in on the deal afterward in that circle I talked about before. I was pissed, really pissed. Especially since they were all laughing at me.

I look back now and I'm sure the morning auction guy was in on it, too. This little episode was going to probably net him around $200, I figured. But I remained calm because it happens and you win some and you lose some at the steps. There were a couple more sales and then the auctioneer took a break.

There's only one auctioneer for the morning sales and sometimes he needs to write up receipts for certain trustees who request that and sometimes he just has to go potty. I heard Jaime say to Jurgen, the German, something about selling him a house. Like maybe he had bought that house and didn't want it. So I asked Jaime if he was going to sell that house he just bought.

"No," he said he didn't think the investor wanted to sell it because, after all, he had bought it for an investor. So, I just took a break with everyone else.

I walked over to the corner and as I glanced across the street, I could see the "good ole boys" standing in a circle. Ah ha, the circle boys. When I saw those assholes across the street auctioning off the house I tried to get fair and square in the auction, I was pissed, seeing all different shades of red pissed. Did I mention that I was half Latina and had the temper to go with it when provoked?

I tell my husband that sometimes when I start to get mad, I can actually feel my blood boiling. Basically, I flew into a rage and ran across the street, holding my phone with the camera application on ready to take photos. I must have looked like a lunatic because when they saw me crossing the street, they started spreading like ants that just got sprayed with bug spray. I wasn't even really that close to them yet.

Once I got all up in their grill, I was snapping pictures ranting, "Smile for the DA, smile for the DA" Ha, ha, ha.

When I think about it now, I WAS a lunatic. I chased

three of them down an alley, ranting and raving, with my pretty little Vera Wang purse flailing from left to right on my arm and my camera outstretched.

Okay, so these grown men, well, I much preferred to call them weasels that day, found an open door in the alley, ran into a restaurant where people were calmly sitting having their lunch. If you can picture these poor patrons having their lunch interrupted by these idiots running into the restaurant, followed by me waving a freaking phone yelling, "Smile for the DA," what the hell must they have thought?

When I got all the pics I needed (like I was really going to do anything with them), I stormed off the other way.

John Little Balls was saying, "Mary, let me talk to you," over and over.

"Yea, you can come talk to me. I'll be in the DA's office, so come and meet me there."

The deal is this collusion and fraud that they pulled was going on every day, but the fact that it was so illegal and they could be in big trouble if they got busted obviously freaked them out.

Now, to complete my performance, I walked down the block to the front of the DA's office. I know, can you believe these jerks did this a block from the DA's office?

I stood there, so mad, calling my husband on the phone to tell him about these antics. I was fuming, but I still found it comical. I was standing there on the phone and I got a call from Jaime. I don't know how the hell he even got my number.

He started saying, "Mary, why you gotta be that way? Let me talk to you." This, in kind of a vato, chicano kind of accent.

I said, "Sure, come over here. I'm at the DA's office." DA being the District Attorney.

He made his way over to me and said he wanted to talk to me where the others couldn't see him. I mean, really, did the guy have any balls or what? We went behind one of the buildings, in the corner of a parking lot, with me still steaming from getting played by those idiots. He explained to me how he wanted to make a deal and sell me the house. Yeah, all of a sudden now he wanted to sell the house to me because he thought he was going to get busted if he didn't.

He told me he'd sell it to me for $10,000 more than

he paid. I told him I had to talk to my partner. So, I went and called my partner and told him I was so fired up and the whole deal that happened. I told him now the little crook wanted to sell me the house for $10,000 more.

"Screw him," my partner said.

I told him, "I completely agree."

We briefly vented about those guys and how they screwed me out of the house and now they wanted to make money on it. I went around the corner where Jaime was pacing and acting like a Mexican jumping bean on Cinco de Mayo. I told him the deal was off and how my partner didn't want it for that price.

After that whole fiasco was over, I was done for the day, so I got in my car and left. I was just getting on the freeway when my partner called me.

"Well, maybe we should have bought it from him, but not for the $10,000," he said.

A little calmer now, I said, "Yeah, maybe for $5,000, because we would have paid that anyway."

He said, "Do you want to call him and see if he'll take $5,000 more than the auction price?"

Now, remember I'd left and was on the freeway going home. I was already thinking about what I needed to do for the rest of the day, but I called Jaime and offered him the five thousand.

"Oh no," he said, he didn't think his investor would sell it for that little. Again with this investor crap, but I played along. That's sort of how it works there. Everyone is bullshitting and everyone else knows everyone is bullshitting because these people are the least credible types around. But we play along like it's the ultimate truth. I think you'd get more honesty at a used car lot like where Kiss Ass Real Estate Agent used to work.

"Well, do you want to ask him?" I said.

"Yeah," he replied. He said he'd ask and call me back.

For some reason, I thought the deal was going to happen, so I pulled off the freeway and waited for the call. Right away, he called me back. Gee, that investor sure was quick. LOL.

"Nope," he told me, "the guy wants $8,000."

"Okay, mmmm, I'll have to call my partner."

I called my partner and he, sensing that we were now in negotiating mode, said, "Offer $7,000."

Hey, I was already off the freeway. I had time. So I called Jaime back and told him. Oh' he just had to call that pesky investor again. Can you see my eyes rolling around here?

He called me back in about two minutes and said, "We've got a deal."

So I schlepped back to the courthouse steps where the auctioneer was doing all the trustee sales receipts for the morning auction. When you win the bid on a house, you give the auctioneer your checks for the amount of the house. For example, if the house was $190,000 and you gave him a check for $200,000, you'd get a refund check back in the amount of $10,000 in about a week from the trustee.

But, if you want to, as he writes up your receipt, you have time to change the checks for a more exact amount, so you've got a few minutes before he actually writes this receipt. To put into perspective how half assed it is, he does most of his receipt writing either right there on the courthouse steps or across the street inside a well known fast food place, the kind that supersizes everything, if you get my drift.

So, Jaime walked in, ordered a burger and told the auctioneer that I was going to take the house instead of him.

The following day when I came back, of course I was all calmed down by this time. I saw John Little Balls and apologized for going all postal on them.

He laughed and said, "You reminded me of a mom of a kid in a neighborhood where all the kids on the street are picking on the kid and the mom comes out of the house and goes ballistic. Yeah," he said, his eyes looking toward the sky in remembrance, "you were like a freaking pissed off mom."

The funny thing is everyone goes through their pissed off moments and it's always for different reasons. One time, a guy who shows up with his brother was screaming like a banshee at his brother because he let a house go when he should have continued bidding. Another time, the Englishman, Winston, was fired up at someone else for going back on his word, apparently in the circle. Gee, that's a shocker. So, every dog has his day and that day was mine.

In the end, I got the house for $142,000 from the auctioneer and paid Jaime $7,000. Fortunately, my bank was a block away. I walked into the bank and got $7,000 in hundred dollar bills for his investor, wink, wink.

I sold the house for $215,000. The really funny thing about this house was because it had been vacant for so long, there were rats living in it. The construction guys said when they opened the garage door from the driveway, all they saw were rats running to and from all corners of the garage. It gives me the creeps just thinking about it. The infestation was so bad that they had chewed through all the pipes in the kitchen and even the sheetrock in the front living room. The rats, not the construction guys.

We couldn't work on the house that way, so I had the guys buy a bunch of traps. They set them out one night with peanut butter, cheese and a smorgasbord of treats. They went in the following morning and all the traps had been snapped, the bait was gone and there were no rats to be seen. I told them to go and buy these units that plug into the wall and put out a high pitched tone. I think the rats moved out once we put those in because we never saw any evidence of them after that. It ended up being a great buy and was affectionately known from then on as the rat house.

## Chapter 9

## DODGING A BULLET

You know how people say it's sometimes better to be lucky than good? Basically, that's what this chapter is all about. When I go the courthouse steps, I usually have a spreadsheet with info on it, like how much I think the house will sell for, fix up costs, any liens or back taxes, etc. That way, I can look at that while I'm bidding and if the bid amount goes over what I was planning on paying, but I really want the house, I can look at my sheet and figure out if I want to go above the amount I was originally going to pay.

You can make those decisions with items that are flexible and within your control. It gets trickier if there are liens or back taxes. I check out liens the city can impose because if the lawn is dead or overgrown, there could be tickets against the house. I call them tickets, but

I don't think anyone else does. Where I live, they start with the first infraction, which is approximately $500.

I bought a house that had numerous 8½ x 11 "tickets" taped to the front door. I think there were four or five of them. The tickets added up to about $2,500. I knew it had a lien because of the dead grass, but I didn't realize they could keep posting them like that just because the city landscape ticket guy has nothing better to do. In most cases, you don't have to pay those, but it's still good to know about them. In buying and selling flip properties, not all surprises are good ones.

Those tickets didn't blow the budget because I always have a cushion, but I've heard of fines totaling as much as $15,000 or $20,000. You can look up the liens in my area at the county recorder's office. They even post them online, but for certain cities they don't show the amount owed. I guess that's because if they want to keep adding fines, they only have to file the lien once. Then, when the title, or settlement company, in some states, goes to work on the escrow, they'll see there's a lien from the city and call to find out the dollar amount.

I don't really know why the city keeps slapping notices on the door, but I would imagine it's just another way they can try to make money and the landscape ticket guy probably needs to justify his job. It seems a lot like selling water after some kind of disaster for $10 a bottle. I mean, they can clearly see the house is vacant and it's not like they're fining the old owner because they, essentially, are gone. I could just see a bunch of old crusty men on the city council coming up with this plan. So every time I see a lien from the city, I make sure we call to find out the amount.

Now, here comes the bullet. The auctioneer had a house for sale that was on my list. The address came up and I bid a penny over. Many times, you don't know what a bid is until the last minute. The bid came up and I looked at my sheet inside my purse. I always have, above or below the final sales price, the maximum for me to pay at the auction. I should say I used to have it there. Can you see where this is leading? The house came up and I bid a penny over. I've bought more than a few houses for a penny over the opening bid amount without any competition. I guess that should have been my first clue when everyone just stood there.

Or maybe when Vince glared at me over his bifocals and asked, "Are you sure?"

I should have stopped and thought about it. It turns out my bid was more than the house was actually worth.

Of course, no one else stepped in and the auctioneer said, "Going once, twice, third and final time. Sold to Mary."

The next few minutes were somewhat of a blur and I'm not sure at what point I figured out I paid too much. I think it was when I put my freaking glasses on and saw that I was looking at the wrong damn column and the amount I paid was the future sales price of the house after I would fix it up and put it on the market.

I'm a pretty tough female. In the industry I've been in for decades, you have to be. I would venture to say that there are more women real estate agents than men, but believe me, they're tougher on their own kind. I'm not a crier, except maybe at sad movies. I'm not one of those whiny women who fret about everything. But on that day, I went to my car and I was on the verge of tears. The only reason I didn't let them flow was because I had to spring into action and see how the heck I was going to get out of this.

I sat in my car, called my partner and explained what happened. Boom, off the phone he went and started calling the trustee's office to see what he could do. Yeah, sure, now he got off his ass when there was potential money loss involved. When I think back on this, I was really upset at the time because I felt I made such a stupid mistake, but even if we had to keep the house and sell it, it would not have been the worst thing to happen. It was vacant, after all. We could have gotten in right away and started working on it and sold it for about the price we paid for it at auction.

Surprisingly, it didn't take long at all for the ball to start rolling.

My partner called me back and said, "You won't believe it. They're going to void the sale."

Whew. *I really dodged a bullet on that one, I thought.*

The trustee's office must have called the auctioneer because by the time I walked back to the courthouse steps with my tail between my legs, he obviously already knew.

"They're going to void the sale," I told him.

"Yeah." He knew already and handed me my checks.

Such advanced protocol for revoking a sale of a couple hundred thousand dollars.

At the end of the day, the first place I drove to was Walgreens to get a $10 pair of reading glasses. I have great long distance vision, but the close up range was failing me. Yuck, I'll just say it. It happens when you get older. There, now you know. From then on, my spreadsheet had the maximum number I was going to pay in bold and separated from the final, fixed up sales price.

The next day when I came back to the courthouse steps, everyone was asking, "Mary, what happened to that sale?"

On the foreclosure websites, you can look up what happened to every house that was on the auction block that day. They post if it was bought by a third party and at what amount, if it went back to the bank, got postponed and so on.

"It shows it went back to the bank," said Harry, throwing his head back and giving me one of those Chinese torture stares.

I'm a practical joker and I love to play them on anyone gullible enough to believe me. Plus, I was feeling sassy since my ass was no longer in a sling.

"I'm not at liberty to say," I answered.

Like I was some freaking special ass agent or

something in cahoots with the bank. Everyone asked me that day what had happened and I gave the same, secret agent answer. This set off a buzz to the day's gossip.

*Geez, they don't know what's going on?* I thought. *And I can't believe these guys really look to see what happens to every house that comes up. When do they have time for that?* I pondered.

I was having a field day keeping my straight face, giving the same answer to the interrogation of Mary. Little did they know I couldn't see my damn sheet and my partner bailed my ass out of that sale. As my dad used to say to me later in his life, "It's hell to get old."

## Chapter 10

## PROFESSIONAL THIEVES

I mentioned before that when the water is off and the smoke detectors are beeping, it's often a sign that the house is vacant... but not always.

I bought a house at the trustee sale that my partner's guy had looked at for me. He told me that the house was empty, although he couldn't see inside because the blinds were closed. At least there were blinds. The kicker for him was he tried the water and it was off, and the lawn was dead, so we knew no one could be living in a house with no running water. I mean, you can't even poop without running water.

After the purchase, I sent him over with a locksmith to change the locks. Then I got a call.

"There's a problem with the house," he said.

He, and the construction guys, always call with that "the sky is falling" attitude.

The construction crew will call and say, "Oh no, the window screens are all ripped up."

"Okay," I'll say, "take them off the windows and put them in our storage. We'll sell the house without screens."

Problem solved.

One time they had me come all the way to a house to show me that the family room cabinets we had ordered for a built-in didn't match the finish of the wood that was already there. I looked at the cabinets and told the crew to take them off and patch up the holes. No one would ever know there was supposed to be cabinets there. Done. I mean, these decisions seem so simple to me, but I guess that's why I get the big bucks.

So, the guy said to me, "We got into the house and there's some furniture here."

I asked, "How much furniture?"

Many times people leave stuff behind. I know a guy who outbid me on a house that was apparently jam packed full of furniture. To this day he doesn't know what ever happened to the old owner. He moved out and left all the furniture and never came back. For some reason, my friend thought the guy might have gone to jail. I don't really know why. He has a dry sense of humor and might have been pulling my leg. In the end, my buddy said he used the furniture to stage houses that he bought from then on.

It's absolutely amazing to me the items we've found in these houses. One time, we found a 50 inch TV. The house was clean and in good condition, and all the appliances were there. There was nothing in the house except for that TV in the front living room. One of the construction workers took it home. Can you imagine how happy his family was when he showed up with that after work? At that same house there was a golf cart in the garage that was left behind. Somebody got that, too. Sometimes we'll take out trailers full of crap left in a house. When I say that, I'm not exaggerating. We had a freaking four wheel trailer that the construction guys hauled around from house to house.

So I tell the guy who got into this house we just bought to put a note on the door and a few days later, some guy called my partner. We gave him the title of CEO. Chief Eviction Officer. I don't know how he did it, but he managed to get people out of these houses with very little resistance and very little out of pocket expense.

The guy who got the note on his door said that he had been locked out of his house. DUH. He gave him some BS story about how he was on a business trip and he just got home and his roommate didn't pay the water bill and that was why the water was shut off. We learned later from the city that the water had been off for a month. He obviously wasn't living there, but he was just trying to get some money from whoever bought the house.

He said he was a tenant and he indeed lived there. We thought that was weird because it was uninhabitable. But, whatever, okay, you're a tenant, what do you want? Cash for keys to the property, he stated. I think he originally wanted $10,000, which was outrageous since he wasn't even living there. The CEO got him to agree to take $4,000 and he would move out. The CEO sent his guy who looked at the houses for us with the money.

This guy he sent had a crappy attitude and a chip the size of Texas on his shoulder. He always pissed off the construction crew and the sub contractors, and believe me, all the parties involved let me know it. I'm convinced this was where the problem started. This guy went over and met the tenant. No one knows exactly what happened, but I would imagine he acted all macho trying to be a big shot, especially since he had a check for $4,000 and basically held all the power over this tenant. Apparently, for some reason, the tenant said he wanted $5,000 instead of $4,000. Probably because our delivery guy pissed him off. Instead of calling anyone, he just told the guy that was all he had and left. At least he didn't give the guy the money without getting the keys. It went downhill from there.

The guy eventually spoke to my partner. My partner was mad that everything didn't go as planned and I guess the "tenant" was pissed as well. Now he wanted $10,000 again. We didn't want to give him that, so we stopped and took a breath to think about everything that had and was about to go down.

At this point we hadn't seen his lease. We knew the guy wasn't living there because of the power and water not being on. I mean, how can you live in a house without being able to take a dump, for Christ's sake? But we had gotten into the house and changed the locks, which is a no-no if someone is living there.

The nature of the tenant, new owner dance is very fragile. The new owner wants to have the tenant move so they can get into the house and start the fix up. The poor tenant is usually just a victim of circumstance, but not in this case. The guy wasn't even living in the house and now he wanted all this cash. Well, we weren't going to give this crook $10,000 because he wasn't even living in the house and when we asked him to provide a lease, he didn't.

Instead, he sicced some gumba attorney from a hole in the wall law firm in San Francisco on us. I think the guy had a post office box as an address. I know the office was a hole in the wall because you know how you can put an address into google.com and see the house and the whole street? I did that on the building he was supposed to be conducting business from and it was one of those kinds of streets where you'd find a bunch of guys with a big garbage can and a fire burning inside it to keep their hands warm. But we checked him out and he did have an actual law license, so we had to respond to him.

I sprung into detective mode and found the old owners. They lived in another city by now. They said they had rented the house about a year and a half ago to the crook's girlfriend, but they never received any rent after the initial deposit. More evidence the guy was a deadbeat. I don't remember who got the homeowner's insurance involved because, by this point, I was on to the next house, but that was eventually the next step.

It took about four months because the crook, the gumba attorney, my partner and the insurance attorney kept going around and around. Finally, in the end, the guy got around $10,000 from our insurance company. While all of this was going on, the house just sat there empty.

The whole fiasco was such a load of bull. We are all for helping tenants with money to move. Hell, we've even given them money AND gotten the whole crew to move them to their new place on a weekend. But the guy wasn't even living there. When a house gets foreclosed, it makes sense that the poor tenant gets monetary help to move on. They usually have paid a deposit and last month's rent that they more than likely won't get back. But this was a total scam job. This wasn't a poor tenant who was getting the shaft. This was a professional crook. He's probably on to the next house by now.

The first few times you're kind of shocked that people can be such liars and professional thieves. My husband says that people are just desperate. In a way, he's right, but being lied to and people thinking they have you by the balls, holding this house that you purchased hostage gets really old. All the excuses and lies and blah, blah,

blah. It toughens you up. I don't know if it's good or bad, but it happens.

One of the worst people we've run into happened to be a local police officer. He owned the house we bought at the auction. We didn't know him, but he told us who he was. When we verified the info, he, in fact, was a local police officer. I went to the house before the auction and met a girl who said she was his fiancée. She knew that the house was going to auction and I asked her if they wanted to stay in the house and we could rent it to them or if they already had plans to move. She called me later to tell me that they indeed wanted to stay and even went as far as to discuss rental prices. So I bought the house enthusiastically, thinking about the future tenants.

When my partner went over to the house after the auction, the guy was there and he was pissed.

You have to understand that these people aren't really pissed at us. Well, maybe they are pissed at us, but they didn't start out being pissed at us. They've been going through crap with the bank that had their loan under scrutiny for months. Sometimes there are two loans on a property and they go through hoops with two banks at a time. They've tried to save their houses, tried to get their loan modified, tried to do a short sale and, for whatever reason, were unsuccessful in all these efforts.

I know a guy who tried to get a loan modification. The bank asked him to send in practically his life history in paperwork. They took their time with it and when they finally got back to him, they said he made too much money and he was declined. So he asked if he could appeal their decision. They said he had to wait two weeks and then he could send his info in again and they would review it. He sent in the exact same info after two weeks and they said that he was declined this time because he didn't make enough money. But he had sent the exact same info! So, I guess my point is, I've heard so many stories where homeowners are getting the runaround that by the time we're on their doorstep, they've had it.

My partner went to the policeman's house and was told he was not paying rent to live in his own f**king house. He was fired up. Somehow, my partner calmed him down, didn't get shot and in the end got him to leave over the weekend! Packed up his whole freaking house and we didn't have to pay him a dime. I hope the cop doesn't read this book because he'll probably come over and shoot me. Anyway, I was on pins and needles waiting to hear from him about what happened.

He called my husband and I and said, "This is your

CEO, Chief Eviction Officer!" The title stuck.

When we purchase a house that may be a little dated, we like to change the light fixtures and ceiling fans. Sometimes the faucets are bright gold and kind of old. We'll take them out and put in brushed nickel faucets. Sometimes toilets might be funky and cracked. They're really cheap and we like to replace them.

I bought a house that was really nice, with a pool and a huge yard. Well, huge for urban California. I think it was 15,000 square feet or something like that. The way the house sat on the lot gave it an ample backyard. We bought the house sight unseen, at least on the inside. But from the front it looked really good. The weird thing was that you couldn't see into the house at all. There were no blinds on any of the windows. They had put up paper on the windows. Mmmmm. That's different. Yeah, well, read on.

After I bought it at the auction, we knew it was occupied because the guy that looked at the house had seen someone going into the house when he drove by. We put a note on the door after I bought it with the CEO's number. Remember the Chief Eviction Officer? So, this girl, who was the previous owner, called him. She was really nice and cooperative, and was willing to get out right away. Wow, that was great. He somehow negotiated to give her a few thousand dollars and she was to give up the keys. Since he was out of town, he told her I would be coming by to get the keys and check out the property.

I called her cell phone and confirmed with her that I would be coming. She was so nice and reasonable. I got there and I'll never forget it. I walked in and there was no furniture. I looked down and I saw no carpet or padding, just bare concrete floor.

I said, "Oh, did you sell the carpet?"

"Something like that," she smiled. Gee, she was so friendly and nice.

I looked up and said, "Oh, and the ceiling fans and lights are gone." Okay. I was having small talk with her and her mother, who was there also. I went into the kitchen and said, "Oh, the appliances are gone. Well, I guess we'll just replace those." I looked around. "Oh, I see all the doors are missing, too, huh?" I went into the bathroom. "Oh, gee, there's no toilet or sink to wash your hands after you go potty." I was such a comedian.

Okay. They had even taken out the medicine cabinet. I mean, the medicine cabinet? I think those are like twenty bucks. So, by this time I was shitting my pants, but I was trying to act real cool, like I saw this stuff all the time in houses.

I was about to leave and I said, "Oh yeah, I always need to look at the pool equipment. Is it still there?"

The mom had the balls to say, "Oh, most of it."

I said, "I'll just take a quick look."

I went outside and looked at the pool. Someone had taken a saw and cut off all the equipment, leaving nothing but some black pipes. MOST OF IT WAS THERE? Are you shitting me? Replacing things in a house can add up, but basically they're pretty inexpensive individually. Like ceiling fans, toilets, pedestal sinks, light fixtures. All of those you can get for under a hundred dollars each. But pool equipment is a different animal. It's really expensive and the most costly of all is the heater. FYI.

I said, "Okay, thank you for showing me and so nice to meet you, you freaking thieves."

Well, I didn't say that, but I was thinking it. I mean, she had told my partner that the house was in perfect shape. She forgot to mention that half of the inside was missing. So, you know how people say sometimes a house has good bones? What they mean is that the floor plan is good, and the walls; custom touches make it a good house. Yeah, this was actually stripped... to the bones.

I got out of there and called my CEO. I said, "Well, you know how we have to pay people to take out all of those old light fixtures and ceiling fans so we can replace them? Yeah, well, we won't have to do that because they're all gone."

He was pissed. Apparently, this sweet girl had told him the house was fine and everything was there. She had expected me to come in and hand her the cash that she had negotiated out of the CEO. He was furious that she had played him... like a fiddle. He was so mad that he said he was going to call her tomorrow. He was too upset to call her now.

"Oh yeah, and all the doors are gone, and the toilets," I added.

Uh oh. Fuel to the fire. He said he was going to wait a few hours and call her because if he didn't, he wouldn't be able to sleep that night. I don't know why, but I was laughing by this point. Something about someone else being mad and someone else getting in trouble gives me pleasure. Ha, ha.

"Oh, and I went and checked and all the pool equipment is gone, too."

Whoo hoo. That was it. He said, "That's it. I'm calling her right now."

I chuckled. "Okay."

He called me back in about five minutes and said, "You can go over right now and pick up the keys and we won't be giving her any money to move."

What??? What the heck did he say to her? Apparently, he told her that she had stolen all those items and if she didn't get out, he was going to call the police and have her arrested for stealing. With the amount she had taken, it was considered a felony. I don't think he really knew that. He just added it for good measure, but it was probably true.

The girl called me shortly after and she was shit scared. By this time it was like nine o'clock at night. She said, "Please come and get the keys right now because the CEO wants the keys tonight or he is calling the police."

Score one for the CEO. The crazy thing about this is that the girl actually worked for a very well known large bank in their mortgage department. I think that's why she freaked out so badly when the CEO started threatening.

I don't know why the windows on that house were covered with paper before we bought it, but I can only imagine that she was trying to cover up the fact that she had taken everything out of the house. Certainly it wasn't for security purposes. All the stuff in the house was already taken! My hunch is it was so she could try and get money from someone who bought the house.

There's no rule of thumb in this auction business. So, this observation comes with no scientific substantiation as well. But... both times I bought houses that had paper on the windows or towels and sheets hung so you couldn't see inside, they had been stripped like that.

I also know of someone else who bought a house that had brown butcher paper on the windows and the place was completely stripped; even the carpet and granite counters were gone. Who the hell takes out granite counters? Can you imagine how heavy those must have been? The funny thing about this house was that the owner who lost the home actually used to work for my husband. He called her the day before the auction and she pretty much told him not to buy it because she completely stripped the shit out of it.

That's a good thing about living in the area. My daughters hate going anywhere with my husband and I because we end up knowing people wherever we go. A small trip to the grocery store for a carton of milk takes us an hour after all the meet and greets.

Often times we'll look at a house that's coming up for auction and we can't tell if it's occupied or not. Sometimes if that house is in the city I live in, I'll drive by on my way home from somewhere after dark and see if the lights have come on or if anyone has come home recently, although that has proven not to be the end all, either.

We bought a house and we weren't really sure about the occupancy. It was a really nice, newer house built in the last few years and it looked like it was in good condition from the outside, except the lawn was dead, of course.

If you're a real estate agent or know one, you can go on the MLS and see past listings on houses by entering the address. Our MLS, or multiple listing service, goes back many years. I saw from the old listing that it was a beautiful house on the inside and the general floor plan, etc. So we purchased it.

I remember this was a very rewarding purchase for me. I arrived at the courthouse steps just as the auction was getting started. I looked around and none of the people who often buy in the areas I do were there! On my way to the courthouse, there was a huge amount of traffic ahead of me. I could see the traffic up ahead, so I slammed on my breaks, shot off the exit and went the back roads. The cars were stopped in their tracks up ahead, so by taking this detour, I thought at least I would be moving, even if that way should take a bit longer.

I learned later that day that apparently there was a guy on the freeway overpass threatening to jump onto the oncoming cars. So, lo and behold, there I was on my lonesome and the first house was the one I went there to purchase. I could hear a combination of angels in my head singing "Hallelujah" and a voice saying, "Go, go, go."

The other bidders who were currently there weren't interested in that city, so old Mary said, "Penny over."

Going once, twice, sold. YES!

But, of course, the ever cool me just stood there and handed my checks to the auctioneer. Uh huh, ain't no thing. I got the house for $30,000 less than what I was prepared to pay for it. Just as I was giving my checks, I casually glanced out the corner of my eye and saw one of my mean competitors running across the street.

"Was that Grant? Was that Grant?" he said. That was the name of the street.

*Ha, ha, ha,* I thought.

Someone told him, "Mary got it."

Oooh, insert many swear words here. I now knew what it felt like to be the cat that swallowed the canary. Oh, wait, there was another guy coming.

"Has Grant gone yet?" he yelled.

"Mary got it for penny over," another piped in.

Insert disappointing statements here.

*Sorry, guys, should have taken the back roads,* I thought.

Sometimes it is better to be lucky than good. And it always pays to be early... which I never am.

So, relishing in my victory, we went to the house and shoot, it was occupied, but we had so much equity in the house, because of my being ahead of the traffic, that it would be fine. So, we found that there was a guy with his wife and kids... well, we never did see the wife and kids staying in the house. We came to find out his occupancy was somewhat vague.

So often with the professional thieves their role is unclear. Are they a tenant? Well, sort of, but half the time we don't see any leases. Are they an owner? Well, sometime after the notice of default gets filed, they grant deed of the house to someone else, which, by the way, doesn't do a darn thing.

Turned out this guy was neither an owner nor a tenant. He was running some scam job trying to have the loan modified and then buy the house from the owner. The whole thing was so confusing that it makes my head spin trying to explain it. From the old MLS, I could see who the listing agent was, so I called him. Well, good thing I was sitting down. This guy who was living in the house had contacted the old owner and she told him that she had moved from the property. I'm sure he scammed some kind of list showing vacant houses on the MLS. I think initially she fell for his line of bull and was trying to let him be the contact point for modifying her loan.

Somewhere along the way, she realized that the guy was a crook and stopped the whole process, but, in the meantime, the guy moved into the house without a lease or even permission, she said. She was totally believable, especially given the inconsistencies of the crook. She had lost the house, so what did she care about making anything up now? Obviously, when it was listed for sale, the real estate agent put on a lockbox with a key inside. That guy probably had someone let him into the house and changed the locks.

At first, he really didn't want to move from the house. In most cases, people who are still in the house when it goes to auction are either a victim of circumstance or just want to get the cash for keys that everyone and his brother now knows about. So, once you settle on an acceptable amount, the process is fairly smooth.

No, he had a lease and he was buying the house, and he was an owner substitute. The guy was claiming to be everything but the builder of the house. We said okay, if you are a tenant, show us the lease. I knew he didn't have one because the old owner never even gave him permission to move in, let alone draw up a formal lease. He told us this, that and the other, but he couldn't provide one. If memory serves me correctly, I think he did send a lease that wasn't signed by the owner. Crooks are funny. Well, maybe funny isn't the right word; ballsy, that's a better description.

This guy didn't look like a typical thug. He was about 5'7" or 5'8" with a very slight build, good looking and very well dressed, so he wasn't scary. He drove a BMW and was actually very pleasant. Through the whole process he never raised his voice or appeared aggravated in any way. We started the tenant eviction process, which he fought in the court system. Then he sort of gave in and wanted $5,000 cash for keys. By this point, it was a month or so after we purchased the house, and we were pissed by his behavior, so we said forget it. Eventually, we got him evicted. It was down to the wire of when he would have to move. I'm sure he found some other poor sucker to scam and moved into their vacant house. I wouldn't be surprised if we run into him again one day in another foreclosed property.

## Chapter 11

# GREAT NEIGHBOR

One of the houses we bought was in a great area, one of the most desirable in the city. I start my story with this because people will act ghetto, even in an upscale neighborhood.

This particular house had a ton of stuff in it. We could see into the house because the blinds were open, front and back. But, once again, smoke detectors were beeping and the water was shut off.

We bought the house at the trustee sale and once our locksmith opened it and let us in, we started looking from room to room and there was stuff everywhere! Not the usual 30-year-old clothes and toys, but expensive items.

This luxurious living is really typical of many of the

foreclosures we see. So many houses are decked out with granite countertops, expensive lighting and plush carpet, built in cabinetry everywhere. It makes sense because people took so much money out of their homes because they were going up in value and bought toys and cars and upgraded the interiors.

One of the things we never do is take anything from the houses for ourselves. Even though we find good stuff that people have left behind, it just doesn't feel right. I don't know if I'm being superstitious, thinking I'll have bad luck, but I never take anything. Legally, we have to go through a waiting period and then we either donate the items or I give them to a friend of mine who owns a consignment store.

In this particular house, we found all kinds of designer sunglasses, like Prada, Gucci and Ralph Lauren. We found brand new Ed Hardy shoes, golf clubs, a couple of refrigerators, a wine cooler, light fixtures, furniture and more. The list goes on and on. We decided to leave everything so we could figure out what to do with it later, when in walked the neighbor from next door.

He was telling us about how the previous owner was his friend and the guy had a high powered job with a home builder and was laid off because they phased out that part of the business. So he lost the house, his wife and kids left him and he was now living in an apartment in another city. I think that was where the truth ended. He told us that, as a matter of fact, he was seeing him tomorrow for dinner. Yeah, that's right, he was coming to his house for a barbeque. He would let his friend know that the house sold. Wow, great for us. Gee, you're gonna see him tomorrow. What a coincidence.

Can you see my eyes rolling? Can you see my tongue in my cheek? Yeah, if so, then you should have been there with us talking to the guy. So, I gave the guy my phone number and I told him to have the guy call me when he came to his house the next day. I even said we could have our construction crew move everything for him, which we've done a few times.

The following day, dinner time came and went. I said to my husband that I was really surprised the guy never called me. Now that I think back about that conversation in the house with the neighbor, I'm not sure if I even asked for the previous owner's phone number, but the neighbor certainly didn't offer it, either.

I went by the house a few days later to see what we would need to do to it and the very helpful neighbor came over again. Now, this guy literally looked like the boy next door type. No shaved head or tattoos. He seemed like a really good neighbor. I told him that the previous owner never called me. He didn't mention anything about dinner. He just said that he had spoken to the previous owner and the guy was bummed when he told him that the house had been sold and blah, blah, blah. He said maybe he would have a garage sale for the guy.

I said, "That would be a good idea."

I told him he should ask his friend for permission, since it was not his stuff and have the friend call me so we would know it was okay. Maybe he could get a percentage for organizing the sale. Aw, shucks, that wasn't necessary, he was just being a good neighbor. Ha, ha, ha. Can you see me laughing my ass off in my chair at this point?

The next day we had our crew go in and move everything to the garage. This was after we had a kid we knew go through and try to separate the garbage from the good stuff.

Now that all that crap, good and bad, was out of the house, we could start working on what we had to do. The crew went in and started working and I got a call from the crew boss. He said that when they opened the garage to work on the house, the neighbor from next door came and took out all the good stuff and moved it to his house! Long pause on my end. I realized that it was really not their job to guard stuff, but I couldn't believe this happened. Meanwhile, I was at the courthouse steps, trying to concentrate and listen for properties that were coming up for auction.

I don't know if people are getting more ballsy, because there are so many foreclosures in our area and perhaps they know the ropes by now. I'm sure people, neighbors, families talk about their experiences and they see all the shit they can actually get away with. It seems like the more houses we buy, the more people see us coming.

I'm a smart person and very well versed in real estate, but in this particular case, I was at the end of my rope and so done with people and their deceitfulness. It was just the wrong day to pull that crap on me. I told our crew boss to call the police. Oh, and by the way, he was telling the construction guys that Mary Ann said he could have a garage sale... with all that stuff. Oh my gosh, talk about a bottom feeder. First of all, I never said that, and second, I never told him to come and freaking help himself to a houseful of stuff. So, we did what we should have done in many cases, which was we got the freaking cops on him. Police don't generally put up with lawlessness. In the city that this happened in, the crime is very low, so they're happy to come out and ruffle some feathers.

They came out and got the guy to put all the stuff back in the garage he had taken it from. Actually, the guy had gone back to work and his wife was home, so our guys moved it right back into our van and trailer and took it to a storage unit. I think the guy was obviously trying to take advantage of the situation and his wife probably shit herself when the police showed up at her door.

In the end, we put everything in storage for the previous homeowner. It took us a couple of months, but we found him and managed to get all his stuff back to him. I never met the guy, but I heard he was grateful that we contacted him so he could get all those expensive items. I don't know if our construction guys who helped him with everything ever told him what a "great neighbor" he had.

# Chapter 12

# THE TENANTS

We've bought a lot of vacant houses, but because of economic changes and the banks postponing so many sales, we've also had to buy houses that were occupied. When you look at the foreclosure website, you can see the mailing address of the owner. Most of the time, if it's an address out of state or in another city and the house is occupied, either the owner has probably moved out of the house, or it was always a rental and there are tenants living in the home.

Over the last couple of years, tenant rights have changed. It used to be that if you purchased a property, a tenant could be evicted with the proper procedure. Currently, if you purchase a home, at least on the courthouse steps, and it's occupied by a tenant, they have the right to continue their tenancy through the term of their lease. What often happens is the new owner will offer them cash for the keys to the house. Basically, cash to help them move.

Depending on a variety of reasons, the tenant can be offered from $2,000 to $5,000 to move within a certain amount of time. What are the varying reasons? Different investors have their own set of systems and rules for themselves. Let's just say the going rate is anywhere between $1,000 and $5,000.

In the beginning of this foreclosure crisis, owners and tenants were offered cash for keys and I personally had people ask me what that was. Now, even the banks are offering cash for keys.

I had a friend who had gone through a lengthy and crappy divorce. I knew they all can be bad, but this one involved kids and houses and jobs and, well, just a lot of crap. The husband had moved and she was stuck in this somewhat rural area alone with the kids. The house kept coming up for trustee sale, but each time it postponed, so over and over again for about a year, she went through the ups and downs of thinking she was going to be moving. To this day, people don't realize that they won't have to move the instant their house sells. She eventually tired of the emotional roller coaster of anxiety followed by relief when her house didn't sell and moved out before the house sold. It sat empty for about a year.

She later met someone through a friend of hers who desperately needed a place to live. I don't know all the details, but this lady was apparently down and out with children, yada, yada, yada.

She told the lady, "You can move into my house, but it could sell any time at the trustee sale because it's in foreclosure."

The lady didn't care. She would at least have a couple of months to figure out what to do. She had been living in an area that turned out to be completely unsafe for her and her children. Basically, my friend didn't know the lady from Adam, but the person who had referred her did.

Now, my friend's house was fabulous. Designer paint, 4,000 square feet, gated community, granite and tile everywhere. When I tell you what she was going to rent it for, remember that this is the San Francisco Bay Area. The going rate would have been around $3,000 a month. She told the lady she could stay for $1,000 a month and the lady moved in. A couple of months later, the house came up for auction and this time it didn't postpone. However, the minimum bid was too high for anyone to bid on, so it went back to the bank.

The bank showed up and, voila, can we give you $5,000 cash for keys, ma'am? And I know the banks aren't like investors who like to work faster than the speed of sound. They fart around and give people top dollar and give them plenty of time to move. One could speculate that it's good PR, or that they just don't move fast. So the $1,000 a month lady moved out and took her $5,000 cash for keys and my friend got nothing. She was bummed because, by the time this all happened, she certainly could have used the money, even though she was the one who chose to leave.

What I would tell people who are letting their houses go is to stay for as long as you can, tenants and owners. Is it the right thing to do? Who the hell can say anymore? People are losing their houses for different reasons.

I digress here, but we recently purchased a property that was vacant and, lo and behold, here comes the next door neighbor to lay out all the dish on the poor guy who lost his house. Apparently, the guy got a divorce at the top of the real estate market. He bought out his wife in the settlement. The couple had the house appraised and it came in at $600,000. To give you an accurate picture, this was a first time owner, starter house in our area. A three bedroom, two bath, 1,400 square foot house. For $600,000! So, he settled with the wife and she took the cash and he stayed in the house with the new mortgage payment.

Two years later, house prices plummeted and when I bought it at the auction, it was worth $235,000. That's one of those stories that makes you cringe. I don't blame the guy at all. I mean $365,000 upside down in a starter home? I told the neighbor at least the wife got something out of it. He said it was all gone, she snorted it all on drugs.

"Oh," I replied.

He went on to tell me about every freaking neighbor on the street. All neighbors do that. Joe's been in his house ten years and May and Ed are original owners... is how it usually goes. People are so funny. I didn't ask about Joe and Ed, but they feel the need to give a rundown on the whole neighborhood.

This particular neighbor said, "Yeah, it's a great neighborhood and everyone is really cool. We have a weekly poker game at one of the guy's house. It's a good game if you don't mind that they play and smoke a little weed at the same time."

Are you kidding me? Too much information, dude. What if I were a cop or a cop's wife? But I guess that's why I get so much info. I'm not threatening at all and I'm naturally friendly. I've always been that way. I really do enjoy standing and talking to someone for an hour about all their neighbors and, by the way, I thought neighbors stopped smoking weed together in the seventies.

Sometimes I think that compassion is the destiny that makes me buy certain houses, instead of say, for example, a circle boy. We had looked at a house that was coming up for auction and no one could tell if it was occupied or not. No one ever answered when we rang the doorbell, so when it came up for auction, I bought it.

On my way home, my partner called me and said that one of the construction crew had put a note with the number to call on the door in case anyone lived there. Apparently, my partner got a call from a woman who was a tenant living in the property and she was very distraught. He said I would be the best one to handle this. Why the hell can men not deal with a crying female?

Anyway, I went to the house on my way home from the auction. The lady was in a chair in the garage with the door open and she was crying and carrying on. I told her who I was and tears were streaming down her face as she told me her story.

As if it wasn't bad enough that the house had gone into foreclosure and someone bought it, she had this story to tell. This was Monday afternoon and I had bought the house in the morning. On Friday, the landlord called her and said that this time he needed to get the rent in cash.

She asked him, "Why? My checks have always been good."

She said that he told her he was having some trouble with his bank and that they were going to hold a check of that large an amount, so he needed to get it in cash this weekend so he could make the mortgage payment. She was telling me this story in between sobs and I was rubbing her arm and patting her on the back so she could get it out. She was a wreck and I was pissed that this scumbag could take advantage of a single mom like this. She didn't have any reason to not agree with the landlord's request, so she got the cash and gave it to him when he came over on the weekend. Then on Monday our guys showed up and posted a note saying that the house had been sold.

I sprang into action.

"Let's go inside and call the police," I told her.

We got on the phone with the police and told them the whole fiasco. They were sympathetic, but said that as long as the guy still owned the house when he received the cash, it was legal. As long as he was the legal owner at the time, which he was because I didn't buy the house until Monday, it was perfectly legal for him to take her money. Legal, yes. Moral, no.

The guy knew that this house he owned was in foreclosure. He probably hadn't made his payments for months, perhaps even years. Then, as a last ditch effort to scam more money out of this poor lady on a fixed income, he had the nerve to ask her for cash instead of a check as she had always given him. She gave me the landlord's phone number and we called him and bitched him out together on his answering machine. He wouldn't dare answer his phone. It wasn't going to do us any good, but we both felt better.

While I was there and she and I were going through this ordeal, her, um, well, her, uh, "daughter" showed up. The "daughter" worked for some kind of wood blind company that was somehow tied to one of the large home improvement stores. She had a ton of makeup on and a deep baritone voice... and no boobs. Are you getting the picture? Once again, I cannot make this shit up. I was fascinated by how her makeup managed to cover a dark, hairy five o'clock shadow and wanted to know what kind of foundation makeup she had on, but I thought asking that might be a bit rude. We ended up giving the tenant a few thousand dollars to rent another house and give a deposit, and helped her move all her stuff with guys and a truck. As far as the old landlord goes, that guy has a lot of bad Karma coming.

This happens all too often when the tenants in a property end up being the victims themselves. They just move in and pay rent on time and one day the bank rep comes and sticks a trustee sale notice on their door. They're usually shocked, but the owner knows exactly what's happening, even if they say they don't. The bank doesn't file a notice of trustee sale after one missed payment, after all. I'm being facetious here.

In this economy, it seems like banks are taking months and months to keep up with foreclosures. There are many, many people who haven't paid their mortgage for months, some even years. I know someone who hasn't made a loan payment for three years. They called the bank to see what they could work out and they haven't been able to find their loan. That's another problem. Banks have been bought and sold and eaten up by larger banks and a lot of paperwork is just missing. But don't get me started on that. The whole thing is a big mess. Especially for tenants who did not do anything to be involved in this chaos.

I was almost a victim of these cunning landlords myself. My husband and I were going to rent a vacation house in Santa Cruz, California. The house looked great on that VRBO vacation website, so I contacted the owner. He was like a car salesman, pushing me to rent the house... today. I got one of those gut feelings that said something wasn't right. I looked up the house address to see if it was in foreclosure. Not only had it been a foreclosure, the process was done and it had already been sold back to the bank and was now an REO or bank owned property. I looked through the property chain of title and this guy did in fact own the house before it was foreclosed on.

I called the guy and explained to him that I failed to mention before that I was a real estate agent with access to these records and I noticed that the house had been taken back by the bank. Ha, ha. Minor detail, buddy. He told me with no shame at all that I was correct. It was an illegal foreclosure.

*Oh, aren't they all?* I thought.

In fact, the day we were to arrive was the day that he was to be evicted from that house! I told you, I can't make this up if I tried. He said that he had an attorney and he was going to court before then, so he was sure he would have it overturned and could I please send him the cash now? Insert image of me with a combination of my mouth hanging open and showing him a lovely middle finger.

Well, since my momma didn't raise no dummies, I declined to send him the cash and instead contacted the website so some poor sucker wouldn't be conned by this slime ball. I even copied the foreclosure info for them that showed who currently owned the house. They replied with some bullshit answer about how the guy told them that he owned the house and that was what they had to go on and they wouldn't be removing the listing.

Obviously, they didn't give two shits about the person who would be forking over their hard earned cash, sipping a latte on the deck of that house when the Sheriff came to kick their vacationing asses out. Sorry, but some things really fire me up. Someone being taken advantage of and someone else looking the other way is one of them so bite me, VRBO. Is it okay to say that?

Another friend of mine lost her house. I know, it's a freaking epidemic, what can I say? She rented a really nice house with a pool for her and her young son, close to his school. I told her before she rented a house she should have me take a look at the foreclosure website and see if there were any foreclosure notices filed on the house. I looked it up for her and nothing showed up for that house, so everything was a go.

She moved in and a few months later, a bank rep showed up knocking on her door to see what the occupancy status was. He gave her his card. He happened to be from a large, well known bank. He asked her a few questions, like if she was the owner or renting the property. She was fairly freaked out and called the owner. Yes, the owner said, she was in the middle of a loan modification. Some banks will agree to do a loan modification, or loan mod as it's nicknamed, usually only if you're living in the property.

Once again, there are so many factors involved in order to get a loan modification, and there's no instruction guide on how to do it. Lately, there have been companies springing up and probably some ambulance chasing attorneys who, alas, have the power to modify your loan, change your principal amount and basically solve all your mortgage problems. So who really knows what the banks are up to, or why some loans get modified and some don't. Why some short sales get approved and some don't.

Sure, there's a lot of speculation involving insurance, FDIC and the actual bank. Different banks have different policies, which, by the way, change like you change your clothes. Do you know how many houses I've bought where the owner says they've been in the middle of a loan modification and this was an illegal foreclosure? Plenty.

I even bought a house one time where the man told me he spoke to the bank rep a couple of hours before the auction. He was completely shocked when he found out it sold at the trustee sale. They had told him no way was it going to sell that day. And then it did a couple of hours later. I felt so bad when I went to tell them I had bought it. The wife was welling up with tears and giving me cookies and milk. I shit you not. They had their granddaughter there, who they were babysitting. They were an elderly couple, which just made things worse. Before you start throwing this book across the room and saying what a biotch I am, here's the other side of the story.

They told me they had been in the house since it was first built and it was well over 25 years old. It was refinanced and all the appraised value was taken out in cash. They had a fabulous pool with a whole solar system that could light up the White House. They had a big RV parked at the side of the house, along with a boat so big you could take it to China... and back. They took all the money out of their house to buy all these toys. No one needed surgery or a kidney or anything like that.

On one hand, I genuinely felt very bad for this couple, but don't you think someone who has been in their house for over 25 years should almost have it paid off? Especially since it was not an upper end property. To put it into perspective, the house was probably worth $50,000 when it was new. At the peak of the market, it was worth around $450,000. They took all that equity out and when I bought it, it was probably worth approximately $170,000. Am I wrong in thinking that these people made bad financial moves and ended up losing their house, and now had a bunch of toys that had also depreciated in value?

In the end, we rented the house to them so they could stay. They were going to try and see if they could get the sale overturned and we were okay with that as long as they were okay with renting the house while they worked on it. It's been over a year and they're still renting the house.

You look back and think what the heck were these people thinking? At the height of the market in our area, starter homes, meaning a three bedroom, two bathroom 1,500 square foot home, was going for around $500,000, give or take a few thousand. My husband and I never even thought twice about buying a house for $500,000 that we could rent for $2,000. It just didn't make financial sense. Your payment would have been around $3,800 a month and the rent you could bring in was around $2,000.

The thing about that time period as far as rentals are concerned was that the pickings were slim in finding tenants. It was so easy to get a home loan that it was the butt of the party jokes. There were certain banks that even mortgage brokers would laugh at, saying all you need to qualify for XYZ company is to have a pulse. So, with so many people being able to qualify for loans, the remaining rental pool were people who were the absolute lowest on the totem pole.

If you're in, or were in, the real estate market at all

during the height of the buying frenzy, you know exactly what I mean. Stated assets (hey, just tell us how much you have, we don't need to see any documentation like a damn bank statement), stated income (oh, no dear, we don't need to see any pay stubs, or if you want just make it up or add a few zeros, we don't look at them anyway). NINA (no income, no assets), was one loan my husband, who is a mortgage broker, told me about. I asked him how the hell banks knew if you qualified. He laughed and said he didn't know, he never did any of those loans.

I can remember many, many of our friends who were making a boat load of money as real estate agents or loan people and buying five, 10, 15 rentals. I still know a lot of them and, unfortunately for them, they've lost them all. For the young ones, it sucks, but if you're in your 20s and 30s, you can come back from that and build your assets back up. I know people in their 60s and 70s who have filed for bankruptcy and lost everything. I don't know how you come back from that at that age. I even know a few people in their 50s who lost their houses and moved in with their parents.

I know I got completely off topic here, but the reason I went through the whole rant about those older people whose house we bought was because we ended up renting it to them so they could stay in their house. I know that they probably still think they're going to be able to stay in their house and that the foreclosure will be reversed.

I've bought well over 200 houses on the courthouse steps to date and I know other people who have collectively bought over 500 houses. In all the stories we have and share, I've never heard of any bank reversing a sale because of an illegal foreclosure. I'm not saying it hasn't been done, but I haven't witnessed it. I've seen a few instances where a sale has been reversed because the owner filed for bankruptcy right before the sale and it wasn't stopped in time. I can count them on one hand, though.

I know a guy who bought a house and at the end of the day, the trustee called him and said they were sending the money back. It seems he bought the house at 1:43p.m. and the bankruptcy was filed protecting the house from foreclosure at 1:41p.m.! I know someone else who got a similar call because there was a lis pendens filed right before the auction. That guy I know was lucky to get his money back because a lis means there is pending action on the property, like a lawsuit, etc, which can sometimes take years to resolve. Meanwhile, you're stuck with a house you can't sell.

The flipping business is good to make some quick cash if you have capital to use, but the real ticket now is rentals. I heard someone say millionaires will be made from this market and I agree. Don't get me wrong, house flipping is a really lucrative business. But buying rentals in this market has the potential to build real wealth.

During the last recession in the mid nineties, house prices tanked and there were no buyers. I remember seeing real estate agents I knew who used to be sporting BMWs and Mercedes. All of a sudden, they were driving clunkers. I remember seeing what used to be a top real estate agent driving a piece of white crap down the street. I didn't even know what kind of car it was supposed to be. I knew things were in dire straits because she was a great agent and had a huge business. But, hey when the market stops, no one can beat it back to life.

## Chapter 13

## IT FINALLY HITS THE FAN

My buddy from the courthouse steps called me on my cell phone pretty early one day. I use the term "buddy" rather loosely. He also happens to be a real estate agent in another city in the same county. I don't work or socialize with him, but I like him. He's a nice guy. I met him at the courthouse steps about a year ago. We would share information on houses that were either coming up or postponed, and so forth. We'd talk about things like if a house was vacant or occupied. Because he was often interested in houses in my city, he would ask me many times about what value I had placed on a house. It's commonplace for people, either before or after an auction, to ask what you think the house is worth.

Back to my buddy and this pressing phone call. I answered the phone and he said that he had something really serious to talk to me about. Wow, he sounded really freaked out and I didn't really know him all that well, so what the hell did he have to tell me? He said that he and his wife were up early, around 5 or 6a.m. Okay, that was the first thing I thought was wrong. I'm a night owl, so I can't imagine why anyone would want to get up before the sun does.

Anyway, they were having their coffee, minding their own business when the doorbell rang at 6:30 in the morning. Apparently they had this courtyard area that had a gate that was locked and the freaking FBI broke it down and were all up in his face at the front door. Well, maybe not all up in his face, but in my mind, that's how I imagined it. He said that there were two of them and they came in and started asking him questions.

If you haven't read that chapter called "Pardon Me, What's Bid Rigging?" maybe you should go back and do so now. Remember the tree they used to go under, which was like 25 feet away from the auctioneer, and have their own fun little auction? The FBI asked my real estate agent friend if he knew anything about a second auction at the courthouse. Oh, no, nothing about that, he said. How about the circle that these guys got in after the original auction? Nope, not that either. By this time, my eyeballs were like saucers as I was sitting there in my pajamas on my couch.

So, apparently they asked him a few more questions about the bid rigging process and other not so kosher practices. You know how they do it in that show Law and Order? They ask basically the same few questions in twenty different ways to get people to slip up. So, this guy, who did know about that circle and had, in fact, in a momentary lapse of judgment, been in that circle, of course said he didn't know anything about any of it. Oh boy, the plot thickens.

The FBI guys, who, by the way, had those freaking jackets like on television that say FBI, said oh, okay, well, how do you explain this then? They then pulled out one of those leather portfolio type things and opened it up. They showed him pictures of the tree, yes, the infamous tree, and the circle of guys under the tree with him in the photos! If I were him, I would have been pooping my pants by now. He said they had pictures of him and the other guys under the tree with everyone's name labeled and even the house address that they were auctioning amongst themselves. As I was gulping my coffee down, the first thing I thought of was the first thing out of my mouth.

"Did you see any pictures of me?" *Please say no, please say no,* I thought.

"NO," he said emphatically.

*Yes!* I thought. Okay then, now to finish the story. I had never been in that circle. I was making a boatload of money doing these flips the legal and right way, so I didn't need to be in that circle with them. Furthermore, I like silver bracelets, but not the kind that are attached together and lock. He said that they knew everything. Isn't that just the FBI way? Darn them. They already know everything, so why do they ask if they already know? I have my tongue in cheek right now. I know why. I haven't watched 559 episodes of Law and Order for nothing.

My buddy said, "They knew all the guys and who are the players, movers and shakers."

Well, this certainly has turned out to be a good story indeed. But I wasn't that close to this guy, so why was he calling and telling me about these FBI people? I'm glad he did because I didn't want to be left out of good scoop like that, but why me?

Well, the day before he and I had been bidding on a house against each other. I pretty much reached the top number I was going to pay, so I said to him, "You can have it," stopped bidding and he got the house. When you win the bid, you give your checks then and there to the auctioneer, as I mentioned before. They often times have other houses to auction, so they keep your checks and continue with the auction.

Sometime after, or in between, during breaks, the auctioneer writes up a trustee sales receipt with the vesting information, like whose name the house is going to be in, the address for the grant deed and any refund you have coming back. On this particular day, there were a few other houses and because my friend wasn't bidding on another house, he had time to go and make a call regarding the one he just got.

I'm not sure if he had someone go to the house and talk to the occupants or if he somehow got the information from someone else, but he came up to me before he had his receipt done. He said that he had a change of heart about the house because he found out it was occupied by a tenant and he had just gotten through an ordeal trying to get a tenant to move out of a house he had bought at the trustee sale.

Usually things like that always work out, but before they do, there's a lot of footwork that needs to be done. It's stressful when you're going through it, so I could relate to what he was saying. I think he originally thought that the house was occupied by the owner and that was easier than dealing with a tenant.

I had missed out on a few houses because they postponed that day, so I was going to leave empty handed, which is always disappointing. He asked me if I wanted to take the house after all. He said that if I gave him a few thousand, I could have it and have the auctioneer put the house in my name and exchange the checks so he could have his back. Sometimes, after you've bid on a house and you don't get it, you look back and wonder if you should have paid a little more and gotten it. There are so many variables that might make the price worth it. Maybe you can clean the carpet instead of replacing it, leave the tile and not put in granite. Whatever the options are, there always seems to be some available. Plus, this was a cute little one story house in a desirable city, and single story houses are very much in demand. I knew that the house was occupied, but I thought it was an owner. If not, I would deal with it.

I agreed and I paid him a few thousand for the house. When we went over to the auctioneer together, something struck me as odd, but I just disregarded it.

He said, "When we do this, you have to give the auctioneer a couple of hundred dollars."

"What?" I asked if we really had to. What was this guy a keno runner? Was this some procedural thing I was not aware of? Ha, ha. No.

"That's just what the guys do," he told me.

Well, priding myself on not being one of the guys, I didn't give him any money. He was the only auctioneer in the morning auction and I figured that it was his job to write up receipts. So what if he had to move his arm twice to exchange the checks? I wasn't into giving him a couple of hundred dollars to do it. He got his checks back, I gave mine to the auctioneer and he wrote up my receipt, "sans 200 bucks." That's French for "no way on the $200."

This innocent little transaction was what he was calling me about. He said that he told the FBI about our deal because, apparently, once he found out that they knew everything, he spilled his guts and sang like a canary. Oh boy. Now he really had my attention, as if he didn't before, but now I started listening intently, the way you do when you stop chewing and hold your breath. He said that the good old FBI told him that what we did was perfectly legal, as long as we didn't conspire to stop and cheat the bank by not bidding anymore. Heck, I was bidding him up to beat the band. No, there was no conspiring. He won fair and square. He just had a change of heart after he won the house.

Looking back, I can understand why he did, because when we went to talk to the occupants about their plans, there was a lot of double talk. The lady said she was living there and was the mother of the owner, but wait, she was a tenant, but wait, the owner was living there, too. But it was a rental, but it was occupied by the owner. You get my drift. He was experienced enough to know that whenever you get fed a line of bull in the first place, it doesn't get any better from there.

It turned out that someone who wasn't living there, who was the sister of the owner, wanted to buy the house and we were all for it, but in the end she didn't qualify because she didn't have the funds to close, even though she made enough money to qualify for the monthly payment. They ended up moving and we fixed up the house, sold it and made a profit.

He said the FBI knew all the players. I can't remember if he told me or someone else did, because this went around like a junior high school rumor does, but I heard that they had some type of a plant or mole. This person had been in the circle and had even paid off some guys in that circle. He said that they weren't going to do anything to him because they could see that he was a decent guy and had made a couple of bad decisions. Well, the latter is true, but as of this writing, they did come after him in the end.

He said that he got a call a few months later from one of the guys who came to his house that morning. He told my friend that he had better get a lawyer because the FBI was calling him in for questioning. I swear, just the thought of that makes me pee a little. In the end, I think there were seven or eight of them who pleaded guilty because, of course, the FBI said if they cooperated they would be easier on them. He went in for the indictment and is currently waiting for sentencing, but they said that he could face up to a year in jail and a fine of $250,000. If you Google Contra Costa County Bid Rigging, you can read about the bunch of them and see I'm not full of bull.

The plot thickens in this story. The FBI had agents in teams of two and three go to all the homes of those within the "circle" at the exact same time that same morning. They basically did the same thing to all of them, although I heard that the bigger players were visited by five or six of them. To this day, they're still in plenty of hot water.

I didn't really ask what had happened to have the FBI pursue this case, because, unless you were freaking

Helen Keller, you couldn't help but see what was going on every day. He volunteered that he thought it had to do with one day I missed when Matthew was handed a check by another bidder. Damn. Why does everything happen when I'm out of town?

Apparently, there was a house that came up for auction in an extremely nice area. The minimum opening bid was around a million bucks. There was a lady there who someone said was from a well known fitness supply company. The guys told me when I came back to the courthouse steps a few days later that she showed up with bling-bling all over her hands and wrists and was totally a balla. That's gangsta for diamond rings and necklaces, and someone with a wad of cash to back them up. See, I told you I'm bilingual.

This lady was bidding on this property because her son or daughter lived in the house and was losing it, so she was saving the day by buying it at the auction sale. So she bid on the property, and Matthew said to her that they were going to bid her up and make her really pay for the house unless she gave them $100,000! I mean, are you shitting me? $100,000 for that? I bet even the highest price hookers who service Senators don't get that, especially in today's economy.

The lady apparently said fine and the auctioneer said going once, twice, sold. The lady then turned around and endorsed a check to Matthew for $100,000, which he distributed to his future cell mates, I mean, other bidders. This wasn't done in a secret ceremony, but right there in front of God and everybody. There were at least 15 people who witnessed it, including the morning auctioneer. The story varies depending on who tells it to me, but, the basics are always the same. That lady somehow ponied up the cash.

After the FBI shake up, I went to the courthouse steps and all the circle boys (I think that's nicer than saying criminals) weren't there. While they were away, the tone was so much nicer and friendlier at the steps. So were the opportunities. We were buying houses left and right. No one was bidding you up for no good reason or adding another bid at the last minute just to cost you more money. We were buying those houses and skipping away with our trustee sales receipts, whistling a happy tune like we had just gotten on a Disneyland ride as soon as we walked up to it without having to wait in a line.

Then a few days later, maybe a week, one of them came back, then another, and another. I told someone I know at the auction that if that had happened to me, I'd be at home crying. I couldn't believe the balls on these guys to come back after that. They didn't all come back though. Only about half have returned. I think, in part, because they were probably agents buying for other people and when their investors found out that they were under investigation by the FBI, they pulled their funds. I think that puts a bit of a damper on your investment when you have it with someone who is under FBI investigation. I'm just saying.

The other weird thing that happened is, remember that guy who was renting out houses that didn't belong to him? He showed up with a smile from ear to ear like that Cheshire cat in Alice in Wonderland. He didn't bid on anything or stay for a long time. He was just there and I wondered what the heck that had to do with anything because he hadn't been there for months and then all of a sudden, the day after all those FBI visits, he shows up? Mmmm.

So, are you wondering what happened to everyone else? Since my real estate agent buddies fiasco, the local paper reported that five or six more pleaded guilty to bid rigging. My buddy told me that his attorney said that it would be hitting the fan big time in a few months, but that's another story.

## Chapter 14

## YOU'RE UNDER ARREST

This is a story that I put off writing until now. I'm not proud of it, but it's got to be told whether I like it or not. I gave you a little insight into the cast of characters who frequent the trustee sales. What I didn't elaborate on was about the one named Barney and his constant picking on me. I'm not talking about someone giving me dirty looks or a snide comment here and there. Oh no, since he's a short guy, it has to be on a much grander scale than that.

For the last couple of years, our buddy Barney has been calling me "fat pig," "the cow," "fat cow," "pork chop," and assorted other names regarding my size. When I'd walk up to the steps, he'd announce, "I smell bacon."

A girl who used to come to the courthouse said to me, "That pork chop would be a cute nickname if he didn't mean it in a negative way."

"Yeah, it's kind of cute," I agreed.

The funny thing, well, nothing is funny about this, but the thing is, I'm not that person who walks down the street and the first thing you notice is their size. Nor do I need to book two seats on an airplane. When I go to the Disneyland rides, I fit perfectly in one chair. Okay, I can see I'm getting a little defensive about this, but I want you to know that these are nicknames that aren't really justified. I'm probably 20 pounds overweight, which my daughters say is mom size. I can deal with that.

When I was telling someone this story, they stopped me halfway through and asked, "Wait, how old is this guy?"

"I know," I said, "it sounds like a kid, right?"

I would say he's pushing 40. Way too old to be calling ladies derogatory names, especially when they're older than him. I mean, I'm someone's mom for Christ's sake.

When I would be at my office and I would tell my colleagues or partner what Barney was calling me or saying to me, they would conjure up all kinds of comebacks.

"Oh, oh, tell him you can lose twenty pounds, but how is he going to grow 12 inches?" was one of them.

"Yeah, I know," I would say.

But I also knew that if I said anything back to him, it wouldn't do me any good. If I made fun of him in front of all of his crew, he'd probably come and slash my tires. Don't think I'm exaggerating. When this next story happened, I made sure to park my car right at the bottom of the courthouse steps.

On this particular morning, Barney was in rare form. I've lived through and had a great time in the 1980s and I know that when someone is bouncing from side to side, anxious, snorting, blowing their nose, using nose spray and glassy eyed, they've had more than just a cup of coffee. That should have been my first clue to just let things roll off my back.

The auctioneer started crying the sale of a house I was going to bid on. He read all the particulars, like parcel number, trustee number and then the street address.

"Penny over," I chimed and proceeded to give him

my checks and my driver's license.

When someone places a bid, the auctioneer has to take their checks to make sure they have enough money to bid, and their driver's license in case they happened to find those checks walking down the street and decided it was a good day to buy a house at the trustee sale. They make sure that the license matches the name on the checks. This is what they call qualifying.

Here I was with my little orange sundress and ballerina pumps just trying to make a buck to keep my kids in college when, all of a sudden, Barney piped in.

"You're not getting this house," he bellowed.

"Uh, okay." I just kept focused on the auctioneer.

He said, "$100 more," which meant he was willing to pay $100 more than my bid. He handed over his checks and his driver's license. He immediately got on the phone with an investor, who he was going to relay the bidding status to.

"The fat pig has the bid. What do you want me to do?" He was talking to someone on the other end of the phone. At the same time he said that, he elbowed me in the back. He was on the step right below me and basically, for all intents and purposes, right up against me because of the shallow step. When it's enough, it's enough and that was as much as I was going to take. He had been calling me a fat pig for the last couple of years, but he never touched me or threatened me physically, until now. I turned around and pushed him off of me by backhanding him in the face.

"You're not going to talk to me like that again." I was furious.

He was shocked. His sunglasses flew off, he dropped his phone, his messenger bag was flying around and he was disheveled.

"I'm going to get the sheriff. I'm getting the sheriff," he kept saying.

*Are you kidding me?* I thought. "Get the sheriff, I dare you, get them. You elbowed me in the back."

Now, remember, we were on the courthouse steps and a lot of court cases go down there, some really high profile cases, so they have sheriff deputies at the entrance to make sure you go through a metal detector and put your purse on the conveyer belt. It's a very important job, to be sure. I'm rolling my eyes here if you can't see me. I wouldn't trust these guys to watch my dog, let alone the whole damn courthouse. As my father would have said, "They're as helpless as the tits on a boar hog." I don't even remember if they carry guns, but it they do, someone should take them away from them because they'd probably shoot themselves by mistake going after someone.

Barney made his way to the courthouse entrance to get the sheriff. I didn't go anywhere because I'd made this bid and I wasn't losing this house after all that hullabaloo. Now, this all happened really quickly. The auctioneer stopped, which never happens. The auction schedule is like an airport with planes taking off and landing. It's scheduled to go at 10a.m., whether you're there or not, so this was surprising. Barney ran over to the entrance and grabbed some half wit, I mean a sheriff deputy, and brought him over.

All of a sudden, there were probably five other deputies, all standing around trying to look as best as they could in their freshly pressed uniforms. The whole place soon developed into a full blown crime scene scenario. I'm surprised those deputies didn't put up that yellow crime scene tape, but it probably wasn't in their manual. The deputies started questioning everyone there, including the auctioneer.

Now just to make it clear to you, no one likes Barney. They all know he's a criminal sociopath currently under investigation by the FBI, but they don't want to be the next "fat pig." That morning, there wasn't a huge amount of people, or witnesses, as I like to call them. My buddies who were there were busy chatting up some girl with incredibly large boobs. During the backhand, they were busy trying to see what would happen if this chick wearing a plunging neckline bent down to pick up a $20 bill, so, for the most part, they were there, but missed the whole damn thing. Men. See what I'm up against?

Then a deputy who looked all of 20 asked me what happened. He had one of those little cop pads of paper and was in the cop stance that made his spiky black hair bend in a little. I explained to him what happened, but I could see that he wasn't buying it. I kept saying he elbowed me in the back.

"Well, do you have a bruise?" he asked, moving his head side to side to access the scene. I saw that this guy had enjoyed a few of his own CSI episodes.

"I haven't looked yet," I replied.

"Can you show me?" he asked.

"Uh, I'm wearing a dress," I said sarcastically.

I felt like I should have looked around for camera crews. Was I being punked? As the guys continued to be questioned, the deputy pulled me into the courthouse. As I walked by Barney, I could see him giving puppy dog eyes to the deputy as if to say, "I can't believe I was assaulted by that mean lady."

Even when I came home that day, my college age daughters laughed, looking at me in my little sundress and over the shoulder purse saying, "Yeah, Mom, you really look like someone who would beat someone up in those little designer shoes."

The deputies really took their time during this questioning. I mean, this was real crime drama happening right before their eyes, so they were going to milk it for all it was worth. I sat inside for a while and was wondering if they were going to start the auction without me. So much time had passed, I was sure it had gone to some shark just waiting for the right time to strike.

Then the head sheriff deputy, who was around 60 years old, came into the area where I was sitting. He apparently didn't guard the purses, but was somehow in charge of the guys who did. He seemed much smarter and more with it than the other spiky haired deputies. Maybe the gel slows down their thought process. He was graying and seemed like, unless someone was shot or cut open, he wasn't going to get really excited. I liked this guy.

"Well," he began, "he wants to place you under citizen's arrest."

You could tell that the sheriff school tells them not to shake their heads in disgust and take sides, but I got the feeling he was definitely on mine.

"This isn't the way I would have handled this if I was him," he added.

I got the feeling that the old guy wasn't the type to be calling women "fat pig," at least not to their face, so the chances of him being in this situation were pretty slim, I thought.

"Are you kidding me?" I said. "But he hit me and I just defended myself," I pleaded.

He acknowledged that, but said that it's usually the person who throws the second punch who gets caught because no one saw the first one thrown.

*Damn those stupid guys for being busy with that girl,* I thought. You'd think they'd never seen a set of boobs before. He informed me that he was going to try and talk Barney out of it, but he seemed pretty intent on it. I got the feeling he was the one who was going to have to do the paperwork and that would definitely take away from his coffee time. I couldn't blame him. Wasn't there a real crime being committed somewhere that he could go to?

So, there I sat with a 20-year-old spiky haired deputy sent there to watch me. I guess so I wouldn't escape. He seemed really annoyed at me, like I was some punch throwing lunatic. I don't know what his problem was. By me causing a scene, I at least got him off purse duty for half an hour. Finally, the geezer sheriff deputy came back with Barney.

Barney came right up in front of me, faced me and said, "Mary Ann, I'm placing you under citizen's arrest."

Then he turned around and went outside. Since everyone calls me Mary at the courthouse steps, the first thing I thought of was why was he calling me Mary Ann? Spiky Hair Deputy got out his trusty ticket pad and wrote me a ticket. It was green and a carbon copy just like when you speed or go through a traffic light.

When I was telling this story later in the afternoon to someone I know who goes to the courthouse steps but wasn't there that day, he said, "Well, it's a really good story, but there's one thing I want to know."

"Oh, what?" I asked.

"Who got the house?" he quizzed.

I smiled and replied, "Me."

I have to tell you, the whole thing rattled my cage a bit. There I was, the auction was over and it was just me with my little green ticket. I needed to figure out what to do. I thought this sociopath was going to be pissed that I backhanded him in front of everyone there except the boob watchers.

At the courthouse steps, it's a well known fact that Barney and his crew break into all the houses. In the beginning, they would just beat in the side garage door, which was a pain in the ass every time you bought a house that they had been in because you had to replace the door and door jam. Lately, though, they developed their skills and at least managed to purchase some kind of locksmith breaking in tools.

But, the point is, I wouldn't put much past this guy, so I was trying to think ahead. I figured if I ended up at the bottom of the San Francisco Bay with cement shoes on, I at least hoped they were designer. And, I hoped that Barney would be the first person to be questioned. But how to seal the deal? Temporary Restraining Order. That's the thing battered wives and girlfriends get when they want to get away from their husbands and boyfriends.

*I think they would give that to me,* I thought. Barney is a lot more dangerous than some of those boyfriends, but, truth be told, I probably weigh more than him. I could just sit on him.

When you hang out at the courthouse, early on it's easy to tell who the criminals, defendants, are and who's defending them. So, I went up to some nerdy looking lady wearing a suit and tennis shoes who was apparently some women's lib lawyer.

"Do you know where I can go to get a temporary restraining order?" I asked, still rattled from my arrest.

She gave me directions and I hightailed over there before Barney could beat me to the punch. I walked in and went to the information booth. It was a really large building with most of the bottom floor going to the ordeal of getting a temporary restraining order. I looked around the room and saw all women with assorted bruises and tousled hair. Most of them had kids hanging off of them or were nursing while they tried to explain their situation to some glasses-wearing county worker with orthopedic shoes.

I asked the booth lady for the appropriate paperwork. She handed me a ten page packet to fill out and then a twenty page packet explaining how to fill out the ten page packet. No wonder some poor women just stay with guys who beat the crap out of them.

*This paperwork is a nightmare,* I thought.

I didn't mean to be glib. I just hate paperwork, but I was determined to get this done. After all, I did win the bid on that house and I was done for the day.

I filled out all my paperwork, including stating that Barney had been calling me a "fat pig" for the last few years, but now it escalated to full blown assault. When I was done, they reviewed my paperwork and I got put into this conveyer belt type of process going from room to room. One of the last ones was a non-assuming door that was labeled Room 101. I hurled the door open and it turned out that Room 101 was a full blown courtroom. The greeter, another one of those purse watching deputies, took my paperwork and asked me to sit down and that I would be called.

The stories I heard waiting for my case to be called is a book in itself. Geez, people have a lot of problems. Someone had a baby and the father got visitation rights, but the new girlfriend said she was going to kill the ex-wife. All the while, the unfortunate looking female judge took it all in, stamping and marking and signing to give out temporary restraining orders. Most of the people were there by themselves without attorneys and she was quite pleasant. The only time she would get huffy was when these attorneys would get up and plead some bullshit case and always ask for more time, your honor, more time. She was always pissed that they needed more time. I was too, what the heck took them so long to get their shit together? You give it to 'em, judge.

She was looking at papers, moving from page to page.

When she looked up with those bag infested eyes and said, "Ms. Isaacson?"

Oh shit, there's my heart. When did it get into my throat?

"Yes, your honor," I said.

I've watched enough Law and Order to know they like

it when you call them that. I was so geared up to state my whole case when she put her stamp and signature on my paperwork.

"Your court date will be July 16," she bellowed with her turkey neck.

*I like her,* I thought. Plus the fact that she was sporting a few extra pounds probably didn't hurt my case much.

Up and on to the next phase of the conveyer belt I went, and another line to stand in. The person behind the freaking bazooka proof window told me again what the date was.

"Will I know then if I've gotten the temporary restraining order?" I asked.

"You've got it now," she said.

She continued to stamp and seal and copy and press all the paperwork when my phone received a text message.

Husband: Do I need to come and get you?

Me: Why do you ask?

Husband: Do you need bailing out?

Me: How do you know?

Husband: My co-worker saw it on Facebook

Welcome to the digital age. Damn that Mark Zuckerberg. And I was all set for my youngest daughter to marry him. I had gotten so flustered being in the conveyer belt, I couldn't even call my husband and tell him he was married to an ex-con. Plus, if I dared to have my phone ring in court, I think they can string you up by your thumbs. I'm just saying.

He said that a co-worker in his office was on Facebook and someone's page said, "Just another day at the courthouse steps, some lady decked a guy." Since I was the only "lady" there that day, he knew it had to be me. I was afraid he was going to be mad at me for putting his Isaacson name on the wrong end of the criminal justice system, but he took it very lightly. I wanted to know what the hell that co-worker was doing all day on Facebook.

For the following day and the week to come, people were calling me and congratulating me. I told each and every one that I wasn't proud of it and, in fact, it was kind of embarrassing. I explained that Barney had been calling me a fat pig for the last couple of years and I guess I just snapped when he hit me. Caller after caller couldn't figure out how I didn't hit him sooner.

One guy I didn't even know who came over from another county to buy a property in our area came up to me and said, "Are you Mary?"

*Oh shit, what did I do now?* I thought.

"Yes," I said.

He put out his hand to shake mine.

"I want to thank you for putting that little bastard in his place," he bellowed in a somewhat gruff voice.

"Uh, oh, well, I'm not proud of it," I said shyly.

"Well, you should be. He had it coming," he said.

*Gee, so you have to be arrested in order to be admired,* I thought. What a society.

Just because people from far and wide were calling me to pay their respects for my new found right hook didn't mean I could relax. I still had that little green ticket to deal with. My husband has a slew of attorney friends and one in particular is our go to guy. He made arrangements for me to see a criminal attorney he knew. When I went to see her and gave her all the gory details, she couldn't believe it. She was another one who asked how old this guy was. I guess it's hard to believe that this kind of behavior can come from someone old enough not to need pimple cream.

She was ready to take on the case; in fact, she looked forward to putting this guy in his place. Meanwhile, even though I had a temporary restraining order and Barney wasn't allowed within 100 yards of me, he showed up every day and walked his skinny ass right by me as if to defy me. Whatever.

So, you might think this is the end of the story, but when you get one of those little green tickets, you have to show up for your court date. I had it postponed a couple of times because I was busy vacationing. When the day came for me to go to my court date, my attorney couldn't make it. She was probably busy with someone who actually was a criminal that day. So, my buddy attorney stepped in to offer his "I object, your honor" attorney talk.

The courthouse I was to go to was in one of those really nice suburbs of San Francisco, the kind with multimillion dollar homes. I expected to find some fancy, regal building half empty because certainly these hoity toity types wouldn't be involved in something like slapping someone silly on the courthouse steps.

When I arrived and found the courthouse, it wasn't a nice building at all. It was in the back parking lot of some crappy Denny's type restaurant, only not so nice because it wasn't a Denny's. There were like 10 parking spaces and people were circling like sharks do when they smell blood, trying to get one of those coveted parking spots.

I found a spot on the street and made my way to the building. There were probably at least 75 fellow criminals already in line to go into the courthouse. What was taking so long was apparently everyone had to go through the metal detector and have their purse go through a conveyer belt.

*I wonder if the same purse checkers are here,* I thought.

I stood in line, waiting my turn, and even if I would have worn my house cleaning clothes and not washed them for a week, I would have been the best dressed and most presentable person in line.

All of a sudden, my buddy attorney came to the line and said, "Where's your docket number?"

I wasn't used to being a criminal so this lingo was foreign to me.

"This is all the paperwork I have," I said. And I showed him my green ticket.

"I'll take that," he said and he left me in line with the criminals.

He, of course, didn't have to wait because he had one of those "I'm an attorney, get out of my way" badges. As if they need one more thing to make them think they're better than us criminals in line, but don't get me started on that.

He came out of the courthouse only a few minutes later to tell me I wasn't on the docket that day. He said I was free to go and he was going to call the district attorney to see if they were going to press charges. Press charges?

He called me later that day to tell me that the district attorney didn't even have the paperwork from the sheriff's who wrote my green ticket. I knew that geezer deputy didn't want to do that paperwork. Either that or Spiky Hair Deputy dropped the ball on it. Maybe he missed that part in sheriff's class. I was just glad to see my tax dollars at work... on a real criminal like myself.

**Chapter 15**

# SHORT SALES

Many houses that are sold by an investor have been updated and renovated, unlike other houses that might be in a short sale or an REO, which is a bank owned property. The houses that are in a short sale may still have the owners living in them, but, if you own a house, you know there's always something to do to keep it up. If you knew you were selling your house and needed to go through hoops to give your whole life story to the banksters, oh sorry, banks, and would not be getting a dime of equity out of it, chances are most people would not keep throwing money around to maintain what they could just leave and not repair. So, in many cases, there's deferred maintenance in these short sale houses.

A lot of the areas in Northern California are really warm and the water is very expensive, so that's the first thing to go. You can't compare a home that has brand new landscaping to one with a dead lawn and weeds front and back.

I've looked at a fair amount of REO properties, meaning they've already come up for auction and they were not sold to a third party, but instead went back to the bank. Some of them are really scary looking.

I saw one listed on the MLS the other day. There was no picture of the house, but the price was right, even though it wasn't in the best of areas. I thought I should at least go take a look at it. I drove down the street looking for the sale sign on the lawn. As I came up to the house, there was that tagging graffiti all over the side of the house and on the garage door. When I say all over the side of the house, I mean ALL over the side of the house, from the roofline to the ground. I'm an art fan and it was really good work, but not on the freaking side of an entire house. The thing was, the house was really nice, although the lawn was dead. It looked so scary I didn't even go in. I've said more than once I'm not getting shot over a house. So how can that compare to a house that has a new lawn so freaking beautiful it looks like carpet and beautiful paint on the outside and front door that a real painter did and not someone in the middle of the night running from the po po? I don't think you can.

In many areas of Northern California, for example, investors will put in granite counters, stainless steel appliances, new carpet and designer paint as standard. This obviously makes a home of this caliber worth more than one that hasn't been updated at all. So the dart throwing begins.

When an owner decides to sell their house as a short sale, they're selling it for less than what their current mortgage balance is. If there's no equity in their home, they make no money on the sale. They don't really care what it sells for. All they need to do is get an offer and get the bank to approve the sale. That's so much easier said than done.

It also gets very tricky when the homeowner has two or more loans on a home, because they need short sale approval from both banks if they're different. In almost every case, the second loan isn't getting anything from the sale, but they're still required to approve the short sale. That has held up so many sales because of the inability to get short sale approval from the second mortgage. The other big deal is this: Remember when I said that the owners have to jump through hoops? To get approved for a short sale, besides having a buyer and a sales price for your house that the bank will need to approve, you'll need to provide a plethora of details on your financial situation, like bank statements, bills, income, your kids and what they freaking eat for dinner.

When this foreclosure thing happened a few years ago, and short sales started popping up, it was taking months and months to get them approved by the bank. I remember houses were in escrow for nine or ten months in short sales. Then the banks got a bit savvier on the short sales and it seemed like they were speeding up the process. Now, if you're successful at getting a short sale approved, it typically can take anywhere from four to seven months to close escrow. But these times are anything but typical, so here's a wrench that's being thrown at people trying to close short sales now.

When I was looking at houses coming up for auction in the past and I saw them on the MLS in a pending short sale, I totally disregarded them and went on to the next one. Chances were they just didn't sell at auction because they were postponed by the bank. Now, I can't even count how many houses I've purchased in the last six months that have been in a pending short sale.

I remember a house I purchased for a rental. I paid $107,000 for the house, which was a great price for a rental property, especially since it rented for $1,350. I stopped at the house in the afternoon on my way home just to check it out. I went into the house and looked it up and down just to figure out how I wanted to spiff it up. As I was leaving the house, I saw this old, old freaking Cadillac like the kind Danny DeVito would drive in a John Grisham movie. It stopped in front of the house diagonally, like when people are pissed off and are going to come and bitch you out or beat you with a baseball bat. Needless to say, this stopped me dead in my tracks.

The door squeaked open and out got this equally old lady who looked like one of those dames from the 1950s with a bleach blonde bouffant hairstyle. I saw smoke all around and for a second I couldn't tell if it was coming from this tuna boat Caddie or from the lady getting out of it. She got out of the car like an old fart gets off a couch, with a lot of moans and groans. She tossed the cigarette she was puffing on to the ground and my heart dropped to my stomach as I was expecting her to be the disgruntled homeowner who just lost her house. I knew I could take her on, but did I really want to bitch slap an old lady today?

She walked up to me and asked if I was the new homeowner. She went on to tell me that she was the real estate agent representing a buyer who was in contract to purchase this house for $155,000 in a short sale. She handed me a tattered business card that looked like it had been in her purse for the last six years. She went on to say she had spoken to the bank that morning and "those bastards" were in the process of approving the short sale. Right away, I kinda liked this gal.

Needless to say, she was shocked that the house had sold at the trustee sale and she had just wasted four months of her time and energy with her client trying to buy this house. She then said her client still wanted to buy the house and would we be interested in selling it. I called my partner to see if he wanted to sell, but this guy has so much damn money and income that he would rather hold the house as a rental than sell it. Once again, I cannot make up this shit or the cast that step in it.

For whatever reason, the banks are selling those at the auction right out from under everyone involved in the pending escrow. So, just think, you go out with your real estate agent for maybe a month of weekends. You finally find a house. You make an offer and it doesn't get accepted. You go out again. You find another house. You make an offer and let's say it does get accepted. Chances are that unsuccessful process would have a few more go rounds, but I don't want to lose you here.

You get the inspections you need for your bank loan. They would probably include appraisal, home, termite and roof inspections. This could easily add up to over $1,200. All inspections are in and now you just have to wait for the approval from the bank or banks if there's a second mortgage. If you have a house that you're selling, you've probably already sold it, or, if you're renting, more than likely you've given notice.

Usually sometime during this process, if the house has a notice of trustee sale date, it will postpone and not come up for auction because the banksters know there's a contract and potential sale. Meanwhile, the seller is giving their life history to the bank. Remember that part? The house might come up for auction a time or two and postpone and then one day, it comes up for auction, but it doesn't get postponed. At the last minute, it comes out with a minimum bid and it's sold at the auction on the courthouse steps. The only person who is happy is the one who bought it at the auction.

The buyer loses the house and all the money they put in trying to purchase it. The listing agent lost the listing and the potential commission. The buyer's agent, who drove around for weeks, maybe months, trying to find the buyers a house, loses the sale. Not to mention the fact that now the buyers are going to be really annoyed with their real estate agent because they lost the house, even though it certainly isn't their fault at all.

The long and short of it, oh geez, what a pun, is that short sales are pretty much a pain in the ass. I'm involved in one right now. The house is completely stripped and torn apart, but I'm not afraid of it. The bank farted around for so long with the offer, I had forgotten I even made it until the agent called me. Then, even though it was months before they got around to it, they gave a deadline of two days to get all the documentation submitted to them.

The listing agent forwarded a fax he received from the asset manager to me that had the list of everything they needed, as well as a handwritten note at the bottom that said... "If I don't receive these by Friday, I will deny this sale. Kristie."

Now you know why I call them "banksters." I was tempted to fax Kristie back and tell her to put our offer where the sun doesn't shine, but, unlike the guys at the courthouse, I think with my big head and delivered everything promptly and on time.

## Chapter 16

# THE LAST WORD

I think people will have different viewpoints about the foreclosure epidemic and maybe it depends on what side of the fence you're looking over. As far as I'm concerned, I can certainly see all sides. I sympathize with the person who lost their job and stability, and the victims of the economy who have seen the equity in their home plummet. What I can't seem to get behind are the people who tried to take advantage of an already failed system by deceiving the banksters and buying homes they knew they could never afford.

To put it into perspective, it's like taking advantage of government services like unemployment or food stamps, even though someone is perfectly capable of working, but they prefer to stay at home and watch soap operas all day. Not to get on a soap box here, but I believe in those services. I think it's great to be able to have those to fall back on when times are tough and a person or family is doing everything within their power to better themselves, but fall on hard times.

What I hate to see is people taking advantage of the "system." It's the same premise with regards to the foreclosure epidemic. These benefits have been put into place over the last few years to help people who need it to get out of a jam, not for some to use to work the system.

I remember one time last summer, some guy drove by the courthouse and all the bidders were on the steps. He rolled down his windows and began yelling obscenities at all of us. I can't even remember what he said, but he went down the street, turned around, came back and did it again.

After that temporary commotion, Big Tall Walt started flapping his jaw about how someone was going to come here one day and shoot us all up...

"Except for the black people" he said.

I remember we were all laughing hysterically at his story. I don't really know why or what the heck he meant, but he could tell us to look over yonder, there's a tornado coming with such comedy and finesse, I'd be peeing my pants.

I remember saying to him, "What the hell are you talking about? That guy wasn't even black."

He just looked at me and said, "I'm just talkin."

The fact is that over the last few years, I've given business to trades people, like painters, granite layers, landscapers and carpenters, who would otherwise not have had any business because of the economy. Every time I called to give them a job, they were grateful and I was happy to give it to them. I've always preferred to buy homes that were unoccupied so I wouldn't have to tell anyone that they have to leave their home, and if I do have to do that, I know that I'm going to be much more empathetic than anyone else at the courthouse steps.

I think this is starting to sound like one of those "don't hate me because I'm beautiful" speeches. Maybe I've been trying to be too eloquent. What I'm trying to say is, this crap has happened. The freaking banksters would let a damn puppy get a home loan in the year 2005 and when it came in to stamp it's paw on the loan documents, the title companies would have probably given it a dog biscuit treat. The mortgage broker would have told the bank, the puppy makes $10,000 a month rounding up sheep in downtown Chicago and the banksters would have approved the loan.

So maybe everyone is a little at fault. All I know is, when I drive through neighborhoods in my area, there is home after home that is a vacant eyesore with brown lawns. When we buy them and start fixing them up, usually the neighbors come over to tell us what a good job we're doing and they're so happy that this house will look good again and help improve their street.

Saying if it's not me, it would be someone else is sometimes an excuse, but in this case, it couldn't be more true. We're all in this mess together and it's not something we can sweep under the rug. Many of these homes are already vacant. The people who lived there aren't coming back. It's like the inevitable has to happen. This epidemic is something we have to work through and one way is by putting a large number of homes through the foreclosure process, people buying them, fixing them up and reselling them. I'm just trying to do my part and get two kids through college. So, in closing, I guess after all that, what I'm saying is, "Don't hate me because I'm beautiful."

Some days I feel like I could flip and sell the White House, and some days I couldn't decorate a dog house. But, at the end of the day, I managed to put those kids through college and have never felt so empowered and strong. Through this journey that I'm still on, I've stepped in shit, felt like shit and been shit on. After all the gangstas, banksters, circle boys and deceiving partners, I wouldn't change a thing.

www.ingramcontent.com/pod-product-compliance
Lightning Source LLC
Chambersburg PA
CBHW031924190326
41519CB00007B/405